THE KAMAKAS OF WAIKANE,

KANEOHE, OAHU, HAWAII

1816 – 2018

This book is dedicated to

My beautiful wife, Katherine Sachie Cooper

And

Our three sons – Troy, Bradley, Ethan Scott

And

My Loving Mother, Lucy Kapaeloa Kamaka Cooper

As well as to Her Sisters and Brothers

Without whom this book

Would never happen

ACKNOWLEGEMENTS

Many thanks to the readers, my wife, Kathy, and my niece, Ursula, who offered superb insights to the narrative's organization, examples and techniques of storytelling. They stopped whatever they were doing at various times to read the sections I had finished; the amazing thing is that they remembered what they had read previously, so their transition to new sections was seamless.

Many thanks to my nephews, nieces, cousins and the Kamaka family members who rechecked the important biographical data and offered editing comments.

Many thanks to my wife, Kathy, whose artistic skills grace the cover with her original drawing of *Mokoli'i* (Little Lizard); she rescued the cover not only with her line drawing but also suggested the design of the front and back cover themselves.

Many thanks to the supportive Hana staff and team in Honolulu, HI; Wayne, PA; Old Town, Alexandria, VA without whose encouragement and technical tips would have made this publication more challenging.

Finally, many thanks to my energetic designer and publisher, Aislyn Rivera, who put the final touches on this narrative and transformed it into a book.

THE KAMAKAS OF WAIKANE

FOREWORD

This mo'olelo (history) of <u>The Kamakas of Waikane</u> doesn't have a beginning nor an ending; and perhaps it is not a history of the Kamaka *ohana* (family) more than it is a story of characters, some of whom were notable by their achievements, a handful of whom were public figures, a few – not many – of whom spent time in State and Federal prisons, but most of whom lived their lives as decent, honest, caring and hard-working Native Hawaiians who lived, as best they could, their indigenous culture.

In describing who they were and how they lived, the readers, unfortunately, become the victims of the story teller's point of view, research skills or lack of, understatements and stretchers.

There is truth, however, beneath the spin; finding it may take a willing suspension of disbelief, or just being an artful reader who is fascinated by knowing what it may have been like for real people living real lives in a time during which real fairness and equality were not fully evident.

But in all justice, the author assumes the greatest risk by writing and publishing this book; being out of favor by one's own extended family, or even unwelcomed, is certainly not the aim of this narrative.

While there are many nonfictional accounts in terms of family names, locations and dates, it is principally a story of memories recollected in the tranquility of later years; memories faded but strikingly vivid as waves walloping on the walls of the *loko ia* (Fishpond); facts once strongly held but modified by new evidence and opinions.

Telling a story that enthralls, fascinates, captivates and embraces the reader is the aim of this narrative, <u>The Kamakas of Waikane</u>, for what is life if it is unrecorded.

Should anyone be offended, apologies are offered before we start.

What message the reader takes after finishing this narrative depends on where the readers want to go, how they plan to get there, and who can help them get to where they want to go.

So, therefore, we begin as my eldest Grandson, Sebastian Carlo Katsumi Kaleoikaika Cooper, who is seven years old, loves to say, "Once upon a time …"

Table of Contents

Chapter 1. Genealogy

Moela
Husband unknown

Kamala Keaopopoe
Kaohelowahi Kamaka

John Kaoholowahi Kamaka
Annie Emalia Kahonuanuioka'u Aalona Hatton

John K. Kamaka	Annie K. Kamaka
Charles K. Kamaka	Thelma K. Kamaka
Henrietta K. Kamaka	Lucy K. Kamaka
William K. Kamaka	Daniel K. Kamaka
Joseph K. Kamaka	Rachel N. Kamaka
Ronald K. Kamaka	Abraham K. Kamaka

Chapter 2.   Kingdom Days

John Kaoholowahi Kamaka, a Native Hawaiian born about 14 January 1877 during the reign of King Kalakaua, whose mother was Kamala Keaopopoe and father was Kaohelowahi Kamaka, married Annie Emalia Kahonuanuioka'u Aalona Hatton, born at 1880 during the reign of King Kalakaua, whose Great Grandfather was Lyon Baldwin Nainoa, a Judge on the Big Island.

John and Annie were my *Tutukane* (Grandfather) and *Tutuwahine* (Grandmother), respectively.

Little is known of my Grandmother's birth; though my Grandmother was partly white, both she and my Grandfather spoke fluent Hawaiian. My Grandfather grew up in Kualoa, Oahu, the family ancestral lands, moved frequently among Kualoa, Hakipu'u, Waikane and Waiahole, and eventually settled in Waikane when he married my Grandmother.

There is an *oli* (chant), written by a Native Hawaiian family member of my Grandfather and translated by Manu Boyd at the request of Likeke Paglinawan (via my younger Sister, Judy Mae Puahaunani), both of whom were then with the Office of Hawaiian Affairs (OHA), that, among other songs and prayers, describes our ancestors having originally come from the Puna side of the Big Island while a contingent came from the Island of Maui who were somewhat gifted oral storytellers of *mo'olelo* (traditions), respected for their literary skills, but principally noted practitioners of *la'aulapaau* (medicine) who moved sometime at the turn of the 19th century to the sacred lands of Kualoa, Oahu, as competent *Kumua'o La'aulapaau* (teacher of medicine).

Kelikokauaikekai R. Hoe, University of Hawaii-Manoa, published his Master of Arts thesis in May 2004 as a partial fulfillment of the requirements for the degree entitled, "S.E.K. Papa'ai – A Study of the Survival of Maoli Beliefs in Mele of the Nineteenth Century." In his Acknowledgments Section, he mentions:

> There have been many individuals who have contributed to my work on this thesis. First, I would like to express my gratitude to Judy Cooper (added) Tsutsui and the Kamaka

family for their preservation of the text and for allowing me to use it as the focus of my thesis.

The text referred to in his acknowledgments is the same text that I refer to in the above paragraph; the relationship of S.E.K. Papa'ai to my Grandparents is not absolutely clear, but there is a hint of a close relationship as my mother's middle name is Kapaeloa, the same name as Papa'ai's wife who died on February 22, 1879. It is probable that my mother was given the name Kapaeloa to honor Papa'ai's wife.

On page six of his thesis, he writes:

> S.E.K. Papa'ai was born on the island of Hawai'i in the district of Puna in 1826, just six years after the American Protestant missionaries arrived in these islands.
> His father's name was Keone and his mother's was Pi. He also had a sister and a brother. Papa'ai was married on December 1, 1852, to Kapaeloa. She was from the island of Maui, but they were married in Kawaihae on the island of Hawaii. Together they moved to Waikane on the Ko'olau side of the island of Oahu and had two children. K. Manono was their son and was born on January 24, 1854. H. Keli'ilapuale, a daughter, was born to Kapaeloa and Papa'ai on April 12, 1855. A second daughter, Haliaka, died a month after Kapaeloa.
>
> Although Waikane is described as a land in which he was a "*malihini*" (foreigner) in some of Papa'ai's compositions, Papa'ai made it his home for the rest of his life and raised his family there. It is not known why Papa'ai and Kapaeloa moved to Waikane, but at that time in history, O'ahu was becoming increasingly important as a center or government and the economy....Perhaps it was not too drastic a change from the places that they came from on Maui and Hawai'i.

It is within reason to believe that my Grandfather was not only related to Papa'ai but that he left Puna on the Big Island and arrived at Ku'uloa on O'ahu to live alongside Papa'ai and his wife, Kapaeloa, before marrying my Grandmother, Annie.

On page 68 of his thesis, he concludes with the final comments:

> This study has shown that the core *maoli* (native) values and beliefs were kept in this ohana in Waikane, at least in the lifetime of Papa'ai, who lived until the turn of the century. Further study needs to be done on how these values were carried forward from that time until the Hawaiian Renaissance which heralded *"aloha aina"* (love for the land) as one of its central themes, and to the present day as the Kamaka family continues to cherish and protect the *aina* (land) that has become their home and their life, Waikane.

S.E.K Papa'ai's *meles* (chants, songs) that makeup the text describe the conflicts between our Native Hawaiian polytheistic religion and the Christian monotheistic religion; the social climate of the time; the decline of the Native Hawaiian population caused by disease and low birth rate and King Kalakaua's initiative, *Ho'oulu Lahui*, (increase the nation); the strong imagery of horse riders connoting sexual strength, among other descriptions of the period in Waikane.

These meles, though written primarily by S.E.K. Papa'ai, represent the most direct testimony of events that surround the Kamaka family, and thus are presented in this narrative to help fill the gaps in research.

My Aunt, Thelma Kamaka Chung, was a truly talented *kumua'o la'aulapaau* who not only took care of the Kamaka family medically but also was very *akamai* (knowledgeable) of Native Hawaiian herbal medicines; I don't ever recall seeing a physician until I entered the 7th grade at Kamehameha School for Boys in 1954, for my Mother always took us to see Aunty Thelma when we were not feeling well.

Not much is known by me of my Grandfather's life since he passed away on 6 January 1936 before I was born on 12 August 1941.

While he rode a palomino horse named Pali, my Grandfather's service to the Kingdom earned him several parcels of land:

- Nearly 12,000 square feet at 321 North Kuakini Street (now the parking garage for Kuakini Hospital)
- Nearly 3 acres in Waikane, probably as a result of the Great Mahele, where he and my Grandmother raised five daughters and six sons who built their homes and raised their children within a village environment, some of whom currently reside there
- 187 acres in Waikane Valley that were seized in 1994 by the U.S. Government citing the law of Eminent Domain
- Approximately 37,000 square feet two hundred meters down the road from the Waikane family land upon which the eldest daughter, Henrietta Ka'akau, and her husband, William Pahia, built their home and lived until their passing; it is also the burial location of three family graves, one of which is my Uncle, Daniel K. Kamaka, born in 1815 but who died in 1828; and the second of which lies my brother, David Kaleoikaika, who died at birth and for whom I am named
- And scattered undocumented, unregistered lands in Waikane and Waiahole

My Grandfather died before I was born, but I recall seeing an image, or his spirit, of him; it was a picturesque glimpse of him, dark brown, unsmiling, sitting tall in the saddle on Pali, his palomino horse, preoccupied with something, at least he seemed to be starring....but not at me, as he was at a flank to my line of sight. Then he disappeared suddenly, like a mist that moves quickly with the wind, across the family land.

He never appeared to me again.

My Grandfather was a respected and knowledgeable fisherman who worked hard at his occupation; rumors swirled around his generosity; apparently he was part of a group of Native Hawaiians who gifted the land on which currently sits Waikane Congregational Church, helped build the Church and the adjacent Minister's home, and was somewhat instrumental in securing a commitment from the Congregational Church elders to place a full time Congregationalist Minister to lead the Church.

All of this is undocumented, but perhaps true.

He was also unfamiliar and ignorant of the land regulations that were created following the Great *Mahele* (Land Division), discussed in the 1830's during Kamehameha III reign and enacted in 1848; while Grandfather practiced communal trusteeship ownership (sharing of the use of land) of property, the rules that followed the Great *Mahele* required registered titles of ownership, property taxes and forms for the transfer of property, all of which were completely foreign to the vast majority of Native Hawaiian commoners at that time.

They were the victims, the uninformed innocents, like my Grandfather, who instinctively understood that, the *Kuleana* (a right) land of 3 acres for which they had to register as a fall out of the Great *Mahele*, came at the dispossession of all lands that Native Hawaiians, and my Grandfather, once owned as communal property.

Following his tradition of common ownership, he permitted members of his extended family to live on parcels of land in Waikane and Waiahole, to grow taro, raise chickens and pigs and live off the land.

Some asked his permission to live and work the land; some did not.

But, unfortunately, all who occupied Grandfather's land either traded or sold my Grandfather's land, espousing their rights as legal occupiers, or squatters, to others, and who, then, as purchasers registered the transfer of the land into a title of their ownership.

Hence, land grab was a common practice after the Great *Mahele*.

But my Grandfather went a step further, either encouraged by family members or those in positions of authority and influence since our country had entered a World War, by leasing his 187 acres of land in Waikane Valley, part of the 1,061 acres of the Waikane Training Area, sometime after the attack on Pearl Harbor in 1941 to the United States Marine Corps for less than $2.00 an acre, and who then used the 187 acres to sharpen their shooting skills prior to entering the Pacific Theater of Operations and the campaigns against the Japanese forces during WW II.

In 1976 the lease ended, and the U.S. Marine Corps signaled that they had removed all the unexploded ordnances (60mm mortars, rockets, hand grenades, among others) and ready to return the land to our family.

In 1981, my two first cousins, who were also brothers, Stanley and Raymond Kamaka, took it upon themselves to cultivate our Grandfather's 187 acres by plowing several acres with dozers, building an irrigation system, establishing at least six taro patches and planted assorted vegetables.

They uncovered a *heiau* (place of worship), petroglyphs and a *kuahu* (shrine) placed there by earlier Native Hawaiians; and they opened the farm for visits by school children and a place for the homeless.

They insisted I witness their hard work; so I did in fact join them one day in 1984 to see for myself not only their six taro patches, each of which was constructed in a cascading design to accommodate the irrigation system, the *heiau*, petroglyphs, and *kuahu* but also a pile of unexploded rockets that had seeped through the hillside or had been plowed up by their dozer.

I was amazed that they had actually begun to farm the land, placed the unexploded ordnances off to the side, and passionately committed to doing the engineering and labor work principally by themselves.

But in 1984 the U.S. Marine Corps at Kaneohe Marine Corps Station, informed of additional unexploded ordnance, ruled that they could not clean the 187 acres of unexploded ordnance and moved to declare Eminent Domain in 1989.

What was clearly evident to me that day among the taro patches was that both had already shifted emotionally and psychologically to the side of anger and resentment towards an American government who had not honored their agreement, resulting in the unfair, prejudicial treatment of Native Hawaiians, especially towards our Grandfather who acted with a quiet, dignified grace for and towards so many others, particularly our country during its time of prosecuting World War II.

In 1994, after years of legal maneuvers by the U.S. Navy and counter-claims by the heirs, principally led by my Sister, Judy Mae Puahaunani, to return to the Kamaka ohana my Grandfather's 187 acres in the same condition prior to the lease, District Court Judge Samuel King approved the Government's condemnation of the Kamaka family land, declaring in favor of the United States' legal claim of Eminent Domain.

The Federal Government then seized the land, posting notices that unexploded ordnances littered the 187 acres and declaring all 187 acres off limits to all with appropriate punishment for trespassers.

The final blow came when the Federal Government sealed the 187 acres within a few weeks after the family signed the legal agreement with a fence around the entire 187 acres; the fence still exists today, though in tatters and hardly in condition to prohibit anyone from entering and farming or living on what was once the Kamaka family property.

It is interesting to note that all the Kamaka heirs received a proportionate share of the $2.099M settlement agreement, approximately $60-150,000 per family, except my first cousin, Raymond Kamaka, who refused to sign the settlement agreement.

On several occasions, he mentioned to me that the United States cannot take away his share of our Grandfather's Waikane Valley property if he did not sign the settlement agreement; he turned the rule of a signature on a piece of document on its head, arguing that without his signature, no agreement can be fully enforced.

And hence prior to his death in 2013, he may have still not signed the settlement agreement.

Raymond believes that a major factor in his spending two years in a Federal prison for tax evasion was the Federal Government's strongly held belief that he tried to undermine the Federal Government, to overthrown the Federal Government, but that is another part of a story to be written by someone else.

Thus, as late as 1994, the benefactors of the Kamaka legacy saw their land taken away by the very entity my Grandfather cooperatively provided his 187 acres as part of his duty to preserve our Nation.

The Kamaka ohana may be the last Native Hawaiians in modern times to have their land ripped out from under them…by the United States.

There is an excellent summary of the this dark episode engineered by the United States Marine Corps published in May 2003 by Environment Hawaii, authored by Teresa Dawson.

My Grandfather's birth is recorded as 1877, and he died on 6 January 1936 at the age of 59; and no one is quite sure where he had been buried or where his *iwi* (bones) rests.

My Grandmother, Annie Kahonuanuioka'u Aalona Hatton, was born in 1880 at Barbers Point, Ewa, as recorded on her ID card; her mother, my Great Grandmother, was Lahela Nainoa who married William A. Hatton; her Great Grandmother, my Great, Great Grandmother, Namahana married Lyon Baldwin Nainoa, a judge on the Big Island.

My Grandmother was issued an identification card by the U.S. Coast Guard on September 13, 1944; she was 64 years old at that time, 5 feet 3 inches, 153 pounds, brown eyes and whose hair was described as graying. Her ID card, serial number A-14-01-12991 but with a C.I.B. Badge Number MO4417, was the property of the Captain of Ports, Honolulu.

My Grandmother's identification card was probably a registration identification for it identifies her as a U.S. citizen and a housewife. I don't believe it was a working pass to the docks of Honolulu or any of the ports of the U.S. Coast Guard in Pearl Harbor or Honolulu.

My vivid recollections of my Grandmother (not my only memories of her) occurred three times, twice at our 7-bedroom family home at 321 North Kuakini Street shared by three families – Aunty Thelma and Uncle George Chung with their six children; Aunty Rachel and Uncle Mickey Uu and their five children; and the Cooper family with six children.

The first time occurred when she gave me $.25 to buy sushi, potato and macaroni salad at the local Japanese lunch stand at the corner of Kuakini and Pauahi Streets.

The second time when she made a banana sandwich with mayonnaise for me as I sat in the red wheelbarrow with the noonday sun providing a burst of warmth. The banana sandwich, with a generous spread of mayonnaise, has come to represent my early days and the Aloha given to me by my Grandmother. It is still my favorite sandwich.

The third time was when I and my sister, Judy Mae Puahaunani, were about ten and seven years old, respectively, spent the summer of 1952 at Uncle Willie and Aunty Ka'akau's Waikane home.

I awoke about 2:00 am in the morning because I heard my Grandmother walking up and down the hallway, almost as an apparition, dressed in a white sleeping gown.

I remember asking my Grandmother, "*Tutuwahine* (Grandmother), what are you doing?"

She replied:

> "Go *moemoe* (sleep); I am waiting for your *Tutukane* (Grandfather); he is coming for me."

Not at all bothered by my Grandmother's response, I went back to sleep on the *pune'e* (couch). When I found her ID card with photo taken in 1944, I shuddered a little as she looked exactly like that when I spoke to her at 2:00 am that morning in 1952.

My Grandmother died shortly after my I fell asleep and was found in her bed by Aunty Ka'akau early that morning, dressed in her white gown.

Then, several weeks after her burial she appeared in my dream as I slept in my bedroom at 321 North Kuakini Street, and asked me to open the front door of the family home so she could come in. I went to the front door and her face appeared in the small window; I hesitated.

The next night my Grandmother appeared once again, this time knocking on the window of my bedroom, asking me to open the window; again, I hesitated.

The next day I told my Mother that Grandmother had visited me twice, both times asking me to let her in the house.

That evening, my Mother slept with me; and my Grandmother never visited or bothered me again.

The sequel to this story occurred during my seventh grade year, 1954, at Kamehameha School for Boys.

Reverend Baird was my religious education instructor, and during one of his classes he spoke about spirits of Saints who watched over those who needed help, and asked for comments; I naturally spoke up and informed Reverend Baird and my classmates about my Grandmother's visits to me, sharing what I thought was supportive of his examples.

That weekend my Father and Mother visited my older brother, Sonny, and me at Kamehameha, bringing our laundry and a cake box of rice, sausage and an egg omelet; we met them in the parking lot adjacent to Paki Hall.

My Mother quietly pulled me off to one side and said:

> "You cannot tell the story of visits by your Grandmother; people won't understand."

Reverend Baird had called my Mother.

Days following I thought about what my Mother had said, neither confused nor angry nor concerned nor worried; for me, it just was.

Born into the Kingdom and lived through the Territory period, my Grandparents never recognized nor understood that they were at the vanguard of the changing nature of the lives of Native Hawaiians.

Waikane was geographically separated from Honolulu; to get to Waikane from Honolulu took more than 3 hours on two-lane roads, including the treacherous Pali Road, especially the initial curve where the wind came at you in tornado-like funnels, oftentimes moving one's car towards the concrete wall that prevented the car from rolling over into the steep valley below, or into a car coming up the Pali Road into the same turn at the same time you were turning the corner.

It was a bit exciting.

And if you happen to drive up or down the Pali Road at night and were carrying pork, the car invariably experienced engine difficulty, oftentimes shutting down completely.

But, then, I never experienced it simply because I refused to place pork in my Studebaker when driving up or down the Pali Road at night.

My Grandparents lived the lives of *maka'ainana* (commoner), or simple folk, though the lineage of my Grandfather suggest a trail of substantial *Ali'i* (Chief) legitimacy, a genealogy that is difficult to disprove. But that is story for a different time.

What certainly is important to recognize for the Kamaka family living in Waikane prior to and at the turn of the 20th century are five factors:

1.   We lived as shared partners with the land and ocean, taking and sharing from our farming and fishing only what the family needed, for we understood that the land was the life giver, supplying all that was essential to sustaining life.

2.   Academic education was foreign but not denied, for nearly all my uncles and aunts attended some level of formal schooling, and my Mother was sponsored by the Judd family through the 7th and 8th grades at Mid Pacific High School, leaving because her father, my Grandfather, needed her to kokua with the requirements of the home in Waikane.

3.   Each of the eleven Kamaka children, my Mother, Aunts and Uncles, built their homes within the 3 acres in Waikane passed to my Grandfather and raised all their children, more than 27 cousins, with a shared philosophy of responsibility, concern and a personal relationship easily established and maintained.

4.   Being somewhat isolated, we knew very little about the changes sweeping through the Kingdom and later the Territory and the country, nor did we care, because we saw little that changed our safe, peaceful, simple unchanging everyday lives. We lived in a village, as it is described today.

5.   While we were proud of the jobs being done by our Uncles, we knew there was a world beyond Waikane, that the one car per day driving by the Waikane Bridge just down from the Tsutsui Waikane Store was a forerunner that change was coming, but we knew we were unprepared to compete in the world outside Waikane.

Uncle John left school at the fourth grade; later he joined the U.S. Navy, came home to Waikane and worked his entire life in construction.

Uncle Charlie never graduated from high school but left every morning with his lunch pail to drive to Kaneohe and start up his riding power mower to cut the grass growing alongside the road from Kaneohe to Waikane.

Uncle Joe was the quintessential farmer dressed in his knee length rubber boots.

Aunty Ka'akau and her husband, Uncle Willie Pahia, were the keepers of the Kaneohe Garbage Dump - he was featured in an article in the daily newspaper, *The Star Bulletin*. Uncle Willie raised chickens and pigs; and he was the best, most knowledgeable fisherman I have ever witnessed.

Uncle William was the elegant Native Hawaiian.

Aunty Rachel remained a housewife her entire life but her husband, Uncle Mickey, was the hardest working Native Hawaiian who simply destroyed the attitude, belief, view held by many of lazy Native Hawaiians.

Uncle Abraham, the youngest and the most vocal, if not articulate, served in the U.S. Army for a very short period, lived his entire adult life in Waikane, and died an alcoholic.

While my Mother dedicated herself to her children until we all left the home and then became a beloved volunteer employee in the two businesses in which she was the principal investor, my Father knew no boundaries to a 365/24/7 commitment to work; he drove himself, he drove the Kamaka family members who grudgingly – absolutely grudgingly – heeded but perhaps disliked him; and he made sure his children, at least the older three (Betty Lou, Sonny, and I), were imbued with the Puritan work ethic - never a day of rest, not even on Sundays.

My entire Kamaka Aunts and Uncles lived in a long, alley-like home situated in the middle of the 3-acre parcel in Waikane, constructed with a porch at one end connecting 7 bedrooms, a bathroom, and at the very end of the tunnel-like home, the dining room and a large kitchen with an ice box that had to be filled each day with a block of ice in order to keep the meats cold.

One half of the home, the back half, was removed when the 3 acres were partitioned into eleven lots of approximately 12,000 square feet each; the front half of the home remained in my parents' lot until they had a Hicks home built in 1953; it was then removed, and with it the last vestige of how the Kamaka family lived.

Except for the language.

My Grandmother, Mother and aunts spoke fluent Native Hawaiian, interspersing English idioms when it better described their story; it seemed to me that my Uncles preferred English with a mixture of Native Hawaiian phrases, but clearly our generation of first cousins was the first wave of modern Native Hawaiians who were pushed, scolded and reprimanded if we did not speak English first; and if we understood but could not orally speak Native Hawaiian, it was fine with my Mother and her generation.

The transformation from the Kingdom days to the modern aspects of the Territorial days began with language.

From our ability to comprehend the written word of the Bible or pages within the covers of books, my generation of cousins became the voyagers of a new "Hokulea," sort of the New Age travelers, but our path likened us to nomads, itinerants and wanderers as we tried to sort out every day living from structured systems of economics, politics, environment and social movements.

The days and events of King Lunalilo's rule, which were of my Grandparents' time, were foreign to the Kamakas of Waikane.

They saw but did not feel the sweeping changes in governance or land ownership or systemic cultural disposition; they had lost their *kapu* (forbidden) system in 1819 when Kamehameha II abolished it by the symbolic act of eating a meal of forbidden foods with the women of his court; their Gods shortly thereafter; their language relegated to songs and hulas; their ohana relationships supplanted by social organizations; the fruits of their harvest and labor, and attachment to the land, replaced by packaged products; their strong warrior culture forced underground, and their myths and legends bundled as promotional visitors' presentations.

The days of my Grandparents living in Waikane were unrelentingly idyllic. The land and the ocean provided for their daily sustenance; they had a semblance of order in their lives; they had the gift of life – the land.

But they did not look beyond the reefs…did not see the crashing of the waves upon the coral reefs; they did not see nor understand the immense surge of changes that had already landed on their beaches and moved inward towards the mountains, suffocating their culture, system of worship, language and traditions.

Even our Native Hawaiian Gods did not see nor anticipated the magnitude of the changes that were coming; and for that negligence, they were abandoned by the Native Hawaiians who replaced the many Native Hawaiian Gods with Christianity.

The Kingdom had been leaderless; the governance and social environment toxic; the economics nonexistent; and the future for Native Hawaiians appeared to be a black hole.

Chapter 3.   Territory, Statehood and Modern Hawaii

The period from the illegal overthrow of the Native Hawaiian Kingdom, January 17, 1893 to the year 2017, a period in which the Native Hawaiians observed the transition from being a Kingdom to being a part of a Territory to Congressional approval making them a member of the 50th State in the Union to the modern era of the 21st century, was full of changes to the economics, public policies, social programs, health care guidelines, environmental doctrines, and political stratagems of Hawaii.

Lots and lots of changes over a period of one hundred fourteen years (114), but nothing was different for the Native Hawaiians, particularly the Kamaka *ohana* (family) in Waikane.

The wave of changes that brought prosperity to so many Hawaii residents bypassed many Native Hawaiians, including the Kamaka family in Waikane, perhaps eluding the indigenous, resident Native Hawaiians simply because, though the most literate group of people in the mid 1800's principally through the reading of the Bible, most were unprepared educationally, culturally, economically, emotionally and psychologically; and hence did not see nor understood what was changing.

But there were extraordinary leaders during this time, some who were not Native Hawaiians but all of whom understood that the dominant culture that was indigenous to Hawaii – the Native Hawaiian culture - had to be protected and preserved; hence, they had been working diligently for many years to anticipate and transition change in such a way that benefitted every citizen of Hawaii.

They were the guardians of Hawaii.

Kenneth Brown, an extraordinary Native Hawaiian leader who graduated from Punahou High School and Princeton University, advised me over a period of many years to build healthy communities as they lead to involved, concerned citizens and communities.

An involved, concerned citizenship endorses emerging leaders; focuses attention to public policies; drives economic initiatives; promotes educational excellence; supports strong family values; fosters the growth of industries industry and stimulates innovative thinking.

Kenny traced his ancestry to Papa I'i, an advisor to King Kamehameha I, but Kenny was the most humble person to walk the earth, gentle as rain falling lightly to bless the passing of a distinguished person, who spoke with his eyes and smile.

As the Chair of Queens Healthcare Systems, he persuaded the Queens Healthcare Board of Directors to finance support programs to alleviate the needs of Native Hawaiians, not only in healthcare but also to sustain their culture and traditions; his family donated the property on which now sits the Lunalilo Home; he personally funded the research and publication of Ku Kanaka, a seminal history of who Native Hawaiians are and their current state of affairs in economics, health, education, environment and governance.

After Kathy and I informed Bob Oshiro of Lunalilo Home's need to finance the renovation of their kitchen, Kenny and Bob Oshiro together persuaded the Queens Healthcare Systems Board of Directors in 1998 to contribute $500,000 to the Lunalilo Home, established by a trust by King William Charles Lunalilo, the 6th monarch of Hawaii, 1873-1874, to help with the renovation of their building and kitchen.

Both visited the Lunalilo Home that morning, and at the conclusion of their visit, Kenny presented the check for $500,000 to the Executive Director, Greg Myer; and he and Bob quietly walked to their cars and drove away knowing they had done a good deed.

Kenneth F. Brown was the most respected voice in the State of Hawaii during the 20th century, for he walked the talk in a humble manner.

Bob Oshiro, a WW II veteran, who not only graduated from Duke University School of Law but also was the Chair of the Democratic Party in Hawaii, Executive Director of Queen Emma Foundation, and Director, Queens Health Care System, was an incomparable mentor to me.

An ally of my Father, who both together were brilliant strategists for Hawaii's Democratic Party, he found time to talk story amid his overcrowded schedule.

And when he spoke, I listened.

He mentioned to Kathy and me that when he was a law student at Duke University School of Law, many of his fellow law students pronounced his last name as O'Shiro...the Irish version of the Japanese Oshiro.

Bob always had a smile when he spoke, softly and in measured phrases.

Gracious and courteous, he was one of a group of five Directors of Queen's Healthcare Systems to whom I briefed the spring 1994 in the paneled conference room on the 23rd floor of Queen's headquarters, at the corner of Alakea and Merchant Streets, Honolulu, Hawaii.

I had asked to meet with Kenny Brown, Chairman; Robert C. Oshiro; Ivan Lui-Kwan; and Bob Ozaki to request a financial grant in order to convene a health care summit in Honolulu of Native Hawaiian, American Samoan and Chamorro leaders which would result in a published report that would be given to every member of the United States Congress, all 535 members, 100 Senators and 435 Representatives.

The report was titled, <u>Pacific Americans and The National Health Care Act – Where We Fit.</u>

Upon the conclusion of my presentation, Bob Oshiro, who was seated to my left, leaned over and asked two questions.

The first question Bob asked:

> "Is your father Big Bob?"

And the second question:

> "How did you come up with the name, Pacific Americans, for the Foundation you founded?"

My answer to Bob's first question was: "Yes to the first question; my Father was a large man."

Bob smiled.

And he quietly responded:

"I was called Little Bob, and your Dad was called Big Bob."

Bob's response stunned me, for I had never known of their relationship.

And as for the second question, I replied,

"Asian Americans, Hispanic Americans, African American, Native Americans; they describe a group of people who are firmly embedded in our country but who are passionate of their cultures; so too are Pacific Americans who are distinguished in our country but rooted in the cultures of the Pacific."

Bob responded with one word, "Brilliant."

Within minutes, the Queen's Board produced a check for a significant amount, and Ivan Lui-Kwan offered office space from his law firm for the production of the report, and later introduced me to Ed Case, the Administrative Attorney who provided an entire suite of offices on one floor for our five member team of Tommy Kaulukukui, Ben Pangelinan, Robbie Alm, JoAnn and myself.

Bob Oshiro died in February 2008; he was 83 years old and a living legend, even more so at his death.

Kenny passed in February 2014, the same month as Bob; he was 95 years old, a unique thinker and significant figure in the political, business and cultural life of Native Hawaiians.

Both made a difference, as their leadership stirred movements within the Native Hawaiian communities that continue today.

By the way, we (Territorial Senator Ben Pangelinan of Guam; Tommy Kaulukukui, VP Community Outreach, Queens Healthcare Systems; Robbie Alm, Senior VP of Public Affairs, Queens Healthcare Systems who suggested the title of the report; JoAnn, our typist, and I) did produce the seminal report which I personally delivered to each member of the United States Congress, all 535 elected officials, in the Fall of 1994.

Another seminal, dynamic Native Hawaiian leader was Kahu Abraham Akaka, born in 1917 and died in 1997; Abraham Akaka was born to be a *Kahu* (Minister).

I recall my conversation in January 1994 with *Kahu* Abraham Akaka who was then the Pastor of Kawaiaha'o Church, Honolulu, Oahu. I had called *Kahu* Akaka in December 1993 and spoke to him regarding the newly formed 501(c)(3) foundation, the Pacific American Foundation, that I believed would be an asset to our Native Hawaiian people.

He said to me:

> "I have been waiting for this phone call for thirty years; can you join me next month, January, at the Coral Ballroom for an awards presentation and lunch; we can talk story after lunch."

We met at the Coral Ballroom, Hilton Hawaiian Village Hotel, for a luncheon in honor of Hawaii's entertainer of the year, Frank DeLima; as I approached *Kahu* at the long Head Table, stopping by to say hello to our former Governor, Bill Quinn, *Kahu* said, "We can talk story in the hallway."

At the conclusion of lunch, *Kahu* and I walked out for a restroom break which is at the *makai* (ocean) end of the hallway; *Kahu* spotted a white, round table with two white wrought-iron chairs at the far end of the hallway, towards *mauka* (mountain).

Kahu touched my arm, mentioning that he was headed for the table; I quickly remarked that the two chairs would be taken by the time we got there; *Kahu* just smiled.

The table and chairs were vacant amid the hundred or so that lingered about in the hallway, catching up with each other's stories, and we plopped ourselves in the chairs.

Kahu looked at me and said, "I have to get my glasses out of my coat pocket so I can read the notes I wrote down after our conversation when you called me in December."

As he fixed his black horn rimmed glasses around his ears, he said,

> "I have to tear this paper in half, for one half is what I need to tell my Doctor, you know you have to tell them everything; and the other half is for you."

As he began to speak in Native Hawaiian, he noticed a quizzical look on my face, and said:

> "Let me translate."

I smiled, but perhaps a grim smile, as I was embarrassed by my lack of speaking and writing the language of my Mother, even though Abe Pi'ianai'a, then a living treasure, taught Native Hawaiian language to us during our 7th and 8th grade years at Kamehameha School for Boys.

After neatly folding the torn half and slipping it back in his coat pocket, *Kahu* Akaka began:

> "In my young days I asked my Tutuwahine (Grandmother), who had not ventured far from her home let alone visit the other Islands or the mainland, why all the Hawaiian Gods were dying."

> My Tutu responded, "Because they did not go to New York City."

I was stunned.

During the 1930-40's, New York City was the center of movements of change, the pinnacle of international and national change in economics, governance, public policies, social programs, political strategy, job creation and change for change sake.

The amazing aspect was that *Kahu's Tutuwahine,* never having been more than a mile from her home in Honolulu, knew instinctively that the Hawaiian Gods had not seen beyond the reefs nor anticipated what was coming to Hawaii's shores.

Kahu interpreted his Tutu's comments in this manner:

> "My Tutu was telling me that our Hawaiian Gods were arrogant, not knowledgeable of the world around them, did not care for the preservation of Native Hawaiians, and thus they died because they were not relevant to the Native Hawaiians."

Kahu continued, saying,

> "I was worried for our people; so I contracted with Booze-Allen- Hamilton of San Francisco to do a research study for Kawaiaha'o Church, answering three questions:
>
> Who we are
> Where do we need to go
> How do we get there
>
> The study was never completed; other things interfered, and I suffered the first of a series of heart problems.
>
> And then you called; I have been waiting for your call all these years."

Kahu then put the half-torn page down on the white table, reached out to grab both my hands, and we prayed.
Somehow we parted, amidst the lingering crowd; and I walked around the Hilton Hawaiian Village in a stupor.

An hour later, I called my wife, Kathy, to share with her the spiritual, but real, experience that *Kahu* Abraham Akaka just shared with me.

While I have mentioned over the past several years this unique, exclusive experience to just a few close friends, the memory of that shared moment with *Kahu* Abraham Akaka impacted my life, and I, in turn, hopefully, the lives of many.

But the lives of the Kamaka family in Waikane during the mid to late years of the 20th century continued, unhampered by changes, unfettered by innovations, unchallenged by new ideas or the voices for equality.

The 27 cousins of the Kamaka family represented a shift towards a more balanced life between land, ocean, legends and new occupations empowered by a more formal education, a more disciplined approach to recognizing and managing change, and a greater involvement in options by seeing more opportunities.

Some were balanced; some were not; that is, passive resistance may be the more correct description.

McRonald Kamaka, or Keli'i, saw the world and knew he had a place in it.

A dynamic first cousin, he sat for a State exam administered at Washington Middle School to qualify for a position as a ground guide for airplanes at the Honolulu Airport; he was not yet interested in becoming a 6'3", 350 pound future world wrestling champion.

Scoring the highest mark on the exam, Keli'i was invited 2-3 weeks later to take the ground guide test at Honolulu Airport as a final confirmation before being hired.

Returning to Waikane following the ground guide test confirmation, Keli'i joined a few of us cousins to relate the results of the test, saying:

"The guy looked at me, shook his head, and said how could you score the highest mark and fail so miserably on the simple ground guide test."

Amid the unending laughter that followed, I knew Keli'i having tested the system unsuccessfully, recognized other options were now available.

Keli'i did go on to become a Heavyweight World Champion in several countries as well as winning several tag team titles, to include being the first non-Japanese title belt holder, the WWA World Tag Team Championship under the name of Dr. Moto with his partner, Mitsu Arakawa, among other partners; and he did win the trophy and title of the PWF World Heavyweight Championship.

Upon his retirement, he returned to Waikane where, with my sister Judy's assistance, he parked a small mobile trailer along the edge of the property, baked malasadas and donuts and sold them to the early morning travelers on their way to work; he had become an entrepreneur.

After a few months as an entrepreneur, he returned to Canada; and sadly, he passed away in July 2007.

Leroy Chung, a first cousin my age, was not a passive person; he taught himself the skills of Taekwondo, striking away at the padded 1x4 that, along with 3 others, held up the open air garage; finished one year at the University of Hawaii, Manoa; enrolled in the Hawaii National Guard Officer Candidate School and upon completion was commissioned a Second Lieutenant; completed Rotary Wing Aviation School at Fort Rucker, AL; became a rotary wing pilot for the Honolulu Police for more than 30 years; and retired as a Lieutenant Colonel from the Hawaii National Guard as a helicopter pilot.

Brigadier General Irwin K. Cockett, US Army, retired, was then the Army National Guard Commander for whom Leroy flew, and upon my mentioning Leroy Chung during a conversation, said,

"He was a sterling person, a superb aviator and a proud Native Hawaiian."

Miguel Uu, an incredibly talented fisherman and an equally gifted person, tilted more towards the balanced side than any other Kamaka cousin.

A highly skilled fisherman adept at throw-net, night fishing and free diving, he was also a certified electrician for the State of Hawaii, retiring after more than 28 years of service.

But he lived the values of a Native Hawaiian, caring and providing for his two granddaughters who are now both graduates of Kamehameha Schools and the University of Hawaii, Hilo Campus.

He and his lovely wife who has since passed, Becky, raised their son and two daughters in Waikane, and later were appointed by the Court as the care providers for their two granddaughters; they devoted their lives to their ʻohana.

When we graduated from high school in 1959, he from Castle High School and I from Kamehameha School for Boys, we were fortunate to be hired by Smythe Van Lines, a household moving company located in the Mapunapuna small business district next to the Honolulu Airport.

After several days of work and returning home to Waikane late each evening, I started my 1950 Studebaker early the next morning, about 5:00 am, waited for him to join me, and when he failed to show, I moved the car 20 or so feet along the road and shouted, "Son, let's go to work."

The response was so funny that we both laugh at it today, nearly 57 years later:

"Nah, I tired. I not going work today."

Son was the first Native Hawaiian that I know of to have fought in Vietnam; he was drafted into the U.S. Army, qualified as an artilleryman, assigned to the 1st Cavalry Division, and hit the ground in Vietnam in December 1965 with his 105mm artillery battalion, 1st Battalion, 21st Field Artillery, the first U.S. artillery unit in the Vietnam War. He did his duty, served with honor, returned home to Waikane, and lives a fulfilling life as a fully retired Native Hawaiian combat veteran on the Big Island of Hawaii.

But there were other Kamaka cousins less inclined to take a full swing at life's opportunities. That there were impediments within our society at that time, obstacles to women and those less educated in formal schools, were significant factors in limiting the available opportunities.

For example, Harriet and Carol, both sisters who were highly motivated and talented people, never had the opportunities to do well, or to learn by failing and then getting themselves off of the floor.

The same can be said of my other first cousins who were equally assertive and exuded the right values of compassion, skill sets, among others – Ulu, Manu, Lehua, Lona, Kekino, Ku'ulei – each ought to have lived their lives in greater contribution to our communities.

They were not provided the same opportunities as others because of the social factors of that time.

But that they were superb parents speaks to their personal beliefs, values and ethics.

And they were each wonderful people and have made a positive impact on others, especially in raising their children to be good, industrious, successful and compassionate persons.

Growing up in Waikane limited the Kamaka family's opportunities, narrowed our vision, filtered what we saw and reinforced our uncomplicated way of life.

After all, what better way to spend a day other than going fishing, climbing the Waikane mountain to pick mountain apples, spending $.10 to watch a 16mm reel full length film at Chang's Store in

Hakipu'u only to wildly run the mile back to Waikane taunting our female cousins regarding ghosts, or talking story about things that were only important to that moment.

In a way the generation of Kamakas, my first cousins, experienced difficulty in breaking away from our parents who were still alive and our role models; we were caught in a vortex of change which we did not understand nor appreciate simply because we had no preparation nor encouragement to think outside the box, or how to think about sailing in unchartered waters as our ancestors had done hundreds of years earlier.

We had become civilized in an uncomplimentary way.

The period from about 1980's to 2017 saw a new generation of Kamaka ancestors who were the beneficiaries of my generation.

Whether we passed on more obstacles or valuable critical thinking skills, they, however, are faced with a dilemma that was asked of me during my April 1991 visit to Kamehameha Schools at the invitation of Dr. Mike Chun, the Po'o Kula (Head of School) of Kamehameha Schools.

I was invited to speak on the topic of "what are the differences between my days at KSB and KS today" to the assembled school, 9th through 12th grades, at 8:30 am in Kekuhaupi'o, a kamaboko-shaped like facility that housed not only the school's basketball court but many other school events, as the recently held Annual Song Contest among the top three classes with a trophy, one for the Girls and one for the Boys, awarded to the Class that earned the highest accumulated score, based on certain criteria, among the judges.

I began with the normal accolades to our Kamehameha School and started to speak to the focus of my chat with them, and that is when I lit the fire, especially among the some of the members of the Senior Class, as I mentioned that because of its maturity and willingness to sacrifice to be a winner, the Senior Class during my days at Kamehameha, knowing it would independent in 3 months, always won the trophy for the highest accumulated score.

The Senior Class wanted to leave Kamehameha a winner, and the Annual Song Contest was their final salute to their parents, ancestors and for each other.

The Senior Class that year, 1991, did not win the trophy for the highest accumulated score.

Later that morning my scheduled had me speaking to the students in the Honors English Program, and having been an Associate Professor of English at the United States Military Academy, I was looking forward to a safer gathering.

I addressed the Honors English Program students in the morning, a group of students in the 10th through 12th grades, and the first question asked by a student was:

> "Are you a Native Hawaiian or not? How can you serve the United States and serve the Native Hawaiian people at the same time?"

I was stunned; the question took my breath away.

I mumbled a rather non-sequitur response that I cannot recall today – it must have been a nonsense answer.

As I thought about the question later that day and the years that followed, I realized that the question burst forth because the Honors Students were pulled in different directions; felt strongly the anger of the modern Native Hawaiians; that the question alluded to the confusing message by their Grandparents that it is better to accommodate without being assimilated; and that the question evoked the incipient, raw antagonism of their parents who had realized and understood the injustices inflicted on them and their fellow Native Hawaiians by the system.

I was not prepared for the question in an Honors Literature class, but I was pleased that the question was asked for what is Kamehameha if it did not encourage the challenging of premises.

The third strike was yet to come; and it came later that afternoon when two apparently senior students stopped me in the hallway at the Girls School and gave me a stern reproach that I should not have reminded them of their loss.

My reply to both of them:

"Did the Senior Class win the trophy awarded   to the best singing class?"

They rushed off.

Since that day at Kamehameha Schools, I am a wiser person, reflecting how prescient Thomas Wolfe was in titling his book, You Can't Go Home Again.

The role of culture has always been the tipping point in any discussion of what it means to be Native Hawaiian. It has been a discussion that both informs and inflames, one in which sides are formed, voices inevitably harden and various, different criteria mandated by multitudes of stakeholders.

It is an issue that keeps returning as a central theme facing Native Hawaiians' future; can you be a Native Hawaiian and an American citizen?

In so many ways over so many years, many of us thought about and spoke to this theme; we are no further along towards a consensus resolution today; perhaps we need to think about this issue from another approach.

We may have framed the question incorrectly all these years and were immersed in making choices that marginalized rather than strengthened our future.

"Can you be modern without losing your culture" is really the question that must be resolved if we are to have a future as Native Hawaiians.

The unification of the Hawaiian Islands by Kamehameha I occurred because of the adaptation of technical advances to fit the tactics employed by Kamehameha. Long before the arrival of cannons, muskets and ships, Kamehameha had developed the tactical maneuver of flanking and encirclement...hold the enemy in place while forces attacked the weak points of the formation.

But it was not until Kamehameha grasped the advantages of cannons and musketry that he realized he could not only hold the enemy in place but also race past those forces to cut off their reserves; the introduction of firepower not only caused havoc and weakened the front lines of the opposing forces but also allowed Kamehameha's select *Lua* warriors to attack key weaknesses of the opposing army.

Kamehameha learned how to use the knowledge gained. The art and science of warfare as practiced by Kamehameha then was comparable to the great tacticians of Europe and Asia.

We adapted to the technology of the time, understood how to use the technology and integrated it into a central purpose.

It may have been the first recorded incident of the Native Hawaiian culture being "modern" and Native Hawaiian at the same time.

In 2002 the Pacific American Foundation undertook a project to develop a curriculum of science, math and engineering based on cultural Native Hawaiian scholarship that would meet the criteria and standards of *No Child Left Behind* as well as be accepted by Hawaii's State Department of Education.

The *loko i'a* (fishponds) became the center of scholarship for the project.

After four years of scholarly research and strict adherence to educational principles, the Pacific American Foundation's project objective - the development of curricula for science, engineering and math by the for use by the teachers from elementary through high school grades - was accepted by the State of Hawaii's

Department of Education for use by its teachers from elementary through high school grades.

This achievement validated the fact that Native Hawaiians had been an industrialized nation long before others arrived through its use of engineering principles, production management and appreciation of bio-security in building, maintaining and sustaining five various forms of loko i'a's to sustain its food production capacity.

The validation of the Native Hawaiian scholarship should then be thought of in the same breath as that of Galileo and Copernicus' achievements to mankind.

We were modern without having a single Western or Eastern or Asian influence. There was knowledge, and more important, there was learning.

In 2004 several Native Hawaiian businesses recognized the special leverage afforded indigenous groups by the Federal sole source contracting vehicle; they developed a business strategy that envisioned long term sustainability through a business infrastructure that incorporated Native Hawaiian values with global outreach in engineering, missile systems, information technology, computer design, network management and security industries.

The Native Hawaiian business leaders embraced the complex contractual rules, assertive business development techniques, advanced cash certified financial management systems, sophisticated capture management practices, and competitive nuances of the industry and began to nurture the form and style of successful contractors.

They added one other value, however, to the modern industries best practices – they wrote their competitive proposals using Native Hawaiian cultural values of leadership and management and formed Hui's (teams) with titles that reflected their spirituality of respect for the land, environment and people.

In order for our Native Hawaiian ancestors to have succeeded, and those of us today to become successful economically, socially and politically, we had to borrow from the world.

But that did not and does not make us less Native Hawaiian.

It made us a modern society because we observed, learned and adapted the best practices and techniques from the East and West to fit who we are; and we created trusts to raise the levels of our *ohana's* (family) educational literacy and creation of wealth that can be used to serve others.

What qualifies the distinction of being Native Hawaiian, as well as modern, is how we govern ourselves through the rule of law, demonstrate our respect for others; express the values as civility, fair play, courtesy, hard work, among others; celebrate our culture and language; share our enjoyment of music, art, and literature … and perhaps even the acceptance of the ubiquitous jeans.

While 49% of Native Hawaiians today reside away from the *aina* (land) of Hawaii, they are not a degree less a Native Hawaiian; the remaining 51% of Native Hawaiians reside in the *aina* (land), and they are no more Native Hawaiian than the 49% who live on the mainland.

And we should be proud of being members of our American society that is becoming a proudly diverse society.

Where else but in Hawaii could a *hapa (*more than one race*)* son of Hawaii be raised and where else but in America could the same *hapa* son of Hawaii become the first *hapa* (African American/Caucasian) President of the United States.

The Native Hawaiians who preceded us understood the world they lived in was but a small section of the world of civilization; and when civilization from the West arrived, they understood that they either adapted and learned or stood inflexible with the real possibility of being marginalized.
Can we be both American and Native Hawaiian?

Yes.

As one of the Fellows of the National Pacific American Leadership Institute summarized at the end of the course in 2001, he urged his Pacific American colleagues to:

> "Keep one foot firmly planted in your Native (Samoan, Hawaiian, Tongan, Tahitian, Chamorro, Maori, Fijian) culture and the other foot firmly planted in our American society – maintain a balance."

And as the Chairman, Hui O Hana Pono, said in his closing remarks to the emerging leaders of five Native Hawaiian companies:

> "Put your own indigenous imprint on the growth of your companies; act with cultural leadership values but think in modern global terms."

I am not quite sure how I responded to the question by the Honors student, but it did flummox me as the question came at me from right field, out of nowhere. I believed then as I do now that we can be both, at the same time, an American citizen with a proud Native Hawaiian heritage.

And I think that is why Bob Oshiro responded with the single, descriptive word, "Brilliant."

My nieces, nephews, second and third cousins, in-laws and related family members now entertain a new movement, a new drive, to not only adapt and adjust to changes in their time, but also to preserve and protect the best aspects of our Native Hawaiian culture, traditions and practices.

Taking to the streets may not be the most effective technique (though at times, necessary) to win the necessary votes to change public policy; using persuasive marketing techniques, combined with economic strength, to effect changes important to the preservation and protection of the Native Hawaiian culture seems to be the right critical path for the modern Native Hawaiians.

Developing leaders who have the willingness and intellectual capacity to use existing laws to bring about required changes through the legal system, and simultaneously engage in developing sustained economic and political leadership, is the only way to achieve what Kenneth F. Brown; Robert C. Oshiro; Kahu Abraham Akaka; Likeke Paglinawan; Myron Pinky Thompson; Toni Lee; Nainoa Thompson and many others have sought, including my Mother:

> "To preserve the Native Hawaiian people, their culture, their language, their traditions, their philosophy of life and to sustain the land that nourishes life."

Chapter 4.   The Uncles - John K. Kamaka, Charles K. Kamaka, Daniel K. Kamaka and Abraham K. Kamaka

I had three unmarried Uncles and one who was widowed. All had not gone past the fourth grade; John served in the U.S. Navy during WW I, and Abraham served in the U.S. Army in 1944.

John K. Kamaka, born in 1898 and died July 6, 1962 and stood 6 feet 2 inches.

Uncle John was unmarried, lived with his sister, Aunty Thelma and her husband, Uncle George, and their six children in Waikane, and went to his construction job every day except Saturday and Sunday when he was doing various projects in the yard, or when not working in the yard, sat in his chair at the front door facing the ocean and enjoyed the sun.

He was the most gentle and somewhat engaging Uncle of all; he seemed to take in all that he observed, never criticizing nor judgmental.

During the summer when I was not working a summer job and would spend time doing our landscaping maintenance, I would lean over the chain link fence that separated our homes and talk story with him; generally it was nonsense chatter, as he seldom asked a penetrating question.

Uncle John was devoted to Aunty Thelma, Uncle George and their four sons and two daughters; he lived with them his entire life, willing his inherited 1/11th parcel of land at his death to Aunty Thelma.

While he would ask me about Kamehameha School, he never volunteered anything about his own student days, except that he did mention that his school days principally involved farming and taking care of chickens and cows.

Uncle John was a quiet man who had served in the U.S. Navy but did not speak at all about his service. I always had a warm spot in my heart for Uncle John, waving whenever I saw him but never engaging him in prolonged conversation, no more than a few minutes or so, as we said all we needed to say in those few minutes.

Because I spent nearly 10 months a year for six years boarding at Kamehameha, I never really got a chance to know Uncle John, but he has always remained a kind and industrious Native Hawaiian, never in trouble with the law, lived a simple life and never was at odds with anyone in the Kamaka family or anyone in Waikane.

Uncle Charlie was even more of a recluse than Uncle John; born in 1900 and died in 1968, Uncle Charlie was married to Rachel Hose of whom I have a vague recollection of, except I recall an Aunty who went out for a swim and drowned about 100 meters distance from the muddy beach that fronted the Kamaka Waikane property.

The drowning happened in 1947 or 1948 and may have been Aunty Rachel Hose, Uncle Charlie's wife. I was much too young to know grief nor the protocols of a memorial service; but I do recall that it was a sad time.

Uncle Charlie, for all the years I knew him, lived alone in a one room, shack-like house, dutifully carrying his lunch pail every morning, Monday through Friday, on his way to work as a City and County grounds maintenance person.

We would drive past him on our way to Kaneohe or Honolulu, wave at him (he never waved back) and just marvel that he was the man, my Uncle, driving the large power mower along the road cutting the grass and assorted limbs. I was thrilled to have an Uncle Charlie.

Uncle Charlie stood 6 feet, smoked a lot, did not own a car, did not have a high school diploma and was not visible on the weekends.

I never saw him nor realized he seldom did anything with or for anyone, except he did share a special relationship with Uncle Ronald, Aunty Doris and their family of 3 boys and 3 girls.

Like Uncle John, he willed his entire 1/11th parcel of land to Uncle Ronald on which his two sons, Albert Alapake and William Kahiwa, built their homes.

Uncle Daniel K. Kamaka, my Mother's brother, was born in 1915 and died at age thirteen in 1928.

I believe he is buried next to my brother, David Kaleoikaika, in one of three graves located adjacent to the mango tree at the home of Aunty Ka'akau and Uncle Willie Pahia, now the home of my brother-in-law, Ralph Mutsuo Tsutsui, who with his wife, my sister, Judy Mae Puahaunanai, and their picturesque daughter, Ursula, lived there until Judy passed away in December 2009.

Muts' home is now the centerpiece of the Kamaka family, the cornerstone of our Kamaka legacy and the basis for the possible revitalization of the entire Kamaka generations.

But the title of ownership to that property is muddy as several of my first cousins have a percentage ownership, not large, but a total of at least 20% of the property is owned by others whom Judy and Muts have tried valiantly over the years to acquire their interests.

It is also where family members are buried.

In 2017 Muts, who along with Judy and our cousin Leroy, had been paying for most of the property taxes for nearly fifty years, fifty years of caring for the property, fifty years of negotiations with other minority first cousin-owners, fifty years of frustration but fifty wonderful years of living on a property with a fantastic view of Mokoli'i, Kualoa, White Sand Beach and the ocean, decided to resolve the issue of multiple owners.

Unless Muts finds a solution or resolves the property ownership before he passes, the State of Hawaii could foreclose on the property for unpaid taxes and conduct a sealed bid sale for the property with the title passing to the highest bidder. After the State collects its property tax amount, the balance will be apportioned to the various percentage owners.

Thus, the single piece of property that holds the title to the Kamaka legacy will be lost, closing a circle that began with the Great Mahele in 1848.

The Kamaka family lineage that began in 1816 with our Great, Great Grandmother, Moeala (whose husband is unknown) will then pass into darkness and oblivion.

Uncle Abraham K. Kamaka, the youngest of my Grandparents eleven children, was born in 1921 and died about 1982 (no records available to confirm his date of passing). He was the most affable, the most engaging, the most communicative of all the Kamaka Uncles, and he was also a die-hard alcoholic.

I can recall days when he was sober, but those are few; he was a good drunk (being an alcoholic is never a good thing), a talkative drunk who was never destructive or hurtful; he just walked up and down Kamaka Lane speaking to his ghosts or sat on the grass chatting with whomever he conjured up.

From time to time he would ask me for a bottle of whiskey or a six-pack of beer; and every now and then I would accommodate him but only after he worked alongside me to weed around the plants or rake the leaves that had fallen from the breadfruit tree. And it gave me an occasion to chat with him.

Leroy Chung, who is married to Martha, offered Uncle Abraham an unworkable car situated along the fence adjacent to Kamaka Lane as his sleeping accommodation; and oftentimes I would find Uncle Abraham asleep on the back seat.

I thought then, as I do now, that since no one had offered to care for Uncle Abraham, neither I as well, the offer by Leroy was sincere and genuine; and I felt relieved that Uncle Abraham had a cover over his head when it rained.

Because we were not many years apart, I related to Uncle Abraham more than I did with Uncle John or Uncle Charlie; and perhaps because he struggled with alcoholism, unemployed with no means of self-support, a wanderer with no star to guide him, and merely existed that I think of him today and wished I did more to help him.

My own Uncle, and I did very little to bring a tiny light of comfort to his existence.

Chapter 5. Henrietta Ka'akaualani Kamaka, 1903– 1997

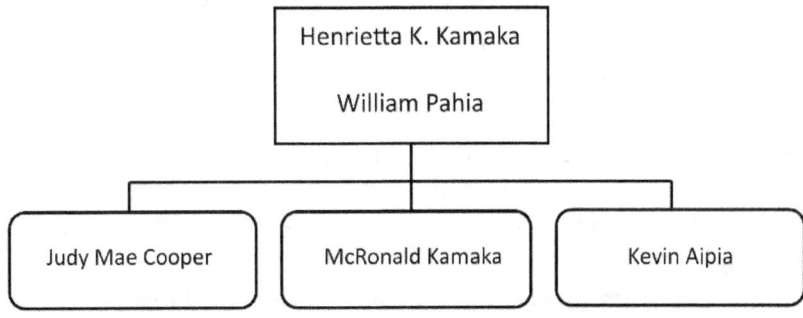

Aunty Ka'akaualani, the eldest of five sisters, was the softest spoken, most gentle and gracious Native Hawaiian lady, second only to my Mother, that I have ever known.

She did not walk – she glided; she did not raise her voice – she just spoke.

Aunty, fluent in native Hawaiian, was also very articulate in English and comfortable with Pidgin English.

As the eldest, she was often spoken of by all of us as Big Aunty.

Uncle Willie Pahia was the consummate fisherman who built a 50 meter pier, anchored on one end at the shoreline just below their home and at the other end a room to place the fishing nets for the three fishing boats moored alongside; just 20 meters on the shoreline from the pier was a fishing shack that housed approximately a dozen Filipino fishermen who took their 4 boats out every day and competed with Uncle Willie, his son-in-law Uncle Charlie Aipia, my first cousin McRonald, and when I was 8 or 9 years old, allowed to join them as a fishing team member but in a minor role – helping lay and pull up the net from the side of the boat.

My sister, Judy Mae, and I spent most of our days and nights on the pier, catching crabs with the round crab nets, affixed by a cord to the side of the pier, that we threw off the pier before the tide rose to the level of the pier.

The crabs that we caught, which we oftentimes threw them into a small fire pit we had started on the shore to cook and eat them, were our lunch and dinner; the Native Hawaiian term for this kind of cooking is called *pulehu*.

There were times when other cousins joined us to live on the pier.

And on one weekend, young Alan Oshima joined us as his parents and our parents were close friends; I am not sure how many crabs we caught that weekend, but Alan and I, who had not seen each other for more than 60 years, suddenly found each other in 2010 in the conference room for Hawaiian Telephone Company and immediately began reminiscing about that weekend on the pier at Waikane.

He also spoke about how his Father in later years would speak with great fondness about my Father. Alan was the General Counsel for Hawaiian Telephone Company at that time, and now he is the CEO and President for Hawaiian Electric Company.

Amazing how weekend crabbing can shape the future.

One day Judy Mae and I were watching the Filipino fisherman place two 12-foot sharks on the entry way to the pier.

I was fascinated as I had never seen such large fishes nor knew they were sharks; I knew I had to touch them because that's what boys did.

Judy Mae hesitated, hung back as I walked boldly towards the mouth of one shark and kicked it on the nose; as the shark quickly snapped to bite my foot, I instinctively jumped back and stepped on the other shark; and luckily I stepped on the backside of his head or I would have lost a foot … or more.

I casually walked away blaming the fishermen for placing live fishes, and sharks to boot, on the entry to the pier; but somehow knowing I had just witnessed a miracle….or dumb, stupid luck.

As I think about it now, that was my closet encounter with two sharks; it was a foretelling of what was to come.

Uncle Willie had built a large room attached to the main house where he kept his nets hanging, spread out on wooden poles that were affixed to wooden horses at both ends; and during the evenings he would patch the nets' broken cords much as a person knitting a sweater, moving his hand-held "needle" through, above and around the broken eyes (cords); I would sit next to him and just observe the process while now and then he would grunt a few words to me which I knew meant to get something for him.

We never talked, but he was teaching me a skill, patiently, as I sat next to him just observing.

It was also in this room that I learned how to make a fish trap out of chicken wire and bamboo, particularly in shaping the mouth that allowed fishes into but not out of the trap.

I was ecstatic as it was something with which I could help him, and when completed, we carried it down to the boat, out to the ocean, and dropped it on the reef with the mouth facing the ocean current since that was how fishes swam, with the current. Uncle placed a colored floater attached to a cord that was tied to the trap.

I asked him as we lowered the trap:

> "Uncle, when we come back in a few days, won't someone else pull the trap and take our fish?"

He looked at me rather exasperated and snapped:

> "No."

I don't believe I ever asked him a question again.

Early every Saturday morning, Uncle and crew would take the boat out to pull the traps and nets, reset both and return home by mid-morning with the catch; by noon Judy and I hopped in the back of the pickup truck to hold the round tubs of fish iced down with ice cubes as Uncle and Aunty drove to Maunakea Street in Honolulu to sell the freshly caught tubs of fish to the Chinese restaurants.

It was a long afternoon as we had to travel up the Pali Road, negotiate the sale of the fish tubs, drive back down the Pali Road and make our way back to Waikane.

After our first trip up and back, Judy and I realized that sitting in the back of the pickup truck may be fun but returning at night was not as entertaining nor exciting.

Unless we had Chinese delicacies to munch on during the drive back to Waikane.

Since Judy was the *hanai* (adopted) daughter, she drew the short straw; but Judy had always wanted to lead, to take charge; and I wanted the delicacies; and as the Saturdays wore on, we become bold enough to ask the Chinese restaurant owners for the delicacies for which Uncle paid, but always at a discount, simply because adults could not say no to children.

Saturdays had become entertaining and exciting because we both got we wanted – she in charge and I my Chinese cookies.

Sometime in his career, Uncle Willie was hired by the City and County to manage the Kaneohe Garbage Dump just up the road from the State Mental Facility. At various times he would take Aunty, Judy Mae and me to the Kaneohe Garbage Dump to help rake the daily truckloads of garbage into the pit; Judy and I were energized as we saw things being thrown away that shocked us; but Aunty would not allow us to remove anything from the site.

I remember her saying:

> "The law says we cannot take anything with us; so just leave the opala."

Later, a newspaper article appeared in the Honolulu Star Bulletin that featured Uncle Willie and his responsibilities at the Kaneohe Garbage Dump; it was his 15 seconds of fame.

During his time as a City and County employee, Uncle and Aunty raised chickens and hens that laid eggs within a chicken wire compound.

Early one morning, Aunty and Uncle were huddled at the front door whispering; Judy Mae and I woke from the *pune'e* (couch) joined them and realized they were talking about a mongoose that had gotten into the chicken wired compound and eating the eggs.

Uncle slipped a rifle to his shoulder, aimed and fired a shot; we all rushed out the front door to witness a dead mongoose, only to find a dead chicken.

A few months thereafter, the chicken raising and egg laying adventure ended. No chickens, no eggs and no mongoose.

In later years I have seen a mongoose up close; and since that morning always wondered why Uncle Willie believed he could hit a mongoose nearly 50 meters away with many obstructions between his line of sight and the mongoose.

After Uncle Willie retired from the City and County, he became a dedicated pig farmer, building two conjoined pig pens to raise pigs, a location at which Judy Mae and Muts now have their duplex apartment.

Uncle Willie became affectionately known as the pig farmer since every day, seven days a week, he would stop by every Kamaka home at 5:00 pm to pick up the leftovers from meals that day and from previous days, food that he fed to his pigs.

He always spent time to chat with my Mother each time that he came by, leaving with a generous laugh that endeared him to us.

My sister Judy Mae was *hanai* in the pure sense of our native Hawaiian culture to my Aunty Ka'akau and Uncle Willie; at Judy Mae's birth, my Mother was in poor health, not expected to survive, and so she asked Aunty Ka'akau to raise Judy Mae as her own in the *hanai* tradition; as such, my sister spent more time at their home than with her siblings at our home.

Except I was privileged to have been the brother who spent my growing years living at their home and sharing with Judy Mae all that was good, noble and kind.

Aunty and Uncle were also *hanai* parents to McRonald (Keli'i), Aunty's nephew, and Kevin Aipia, Uncle's Grandson; and of the three, only Kevin is alive today, living in Waikane with his wonderful family and spending many of his days caring for Muts.

Aunty Ka'akau was in poor health the last 10-12 years of her life; Judy and Muts became her care providers, especially Judy who tended to Aunty's every need, 365/24/7.

Judy was such a strong lady who created her own history, who was event making rather than eventful, who was not afraid to take charge and the responsibilities that came with being in charge.

I was never so proud of my little sister who, unknown to many, had already suffered a heart attack that required a quadruple bypass; yet she put her shoulder to the wheel, kept life moving forward as she cared for Aunty, Muts and Ursula....and all of us, her two sisters and three brothers.

Uncle Willie always celebrated Aunty's birthday with a huge luau at their Waikane home for two days – January 1 and 2.

Preparations began in the summer with drying of he'e, aku, freezing of young white crabs, ensuring the pigs were fed daily, storing of coconuts and keawe wood and canvas and potato sacks, cleaning of the hand-picked river rocks; and finally the day to slaughter and gut the pigs, scrape off the hair using hot water and a sharpened blade, and then hang them upside down from the mango tree to allow the blood to flow into the pans for an evening.

My Aunts and others assembled and prepared the tables both in the adjacent fishing room and out on the lawn while Keli'i was responsible for mixing the poi, Aunty Ka'akau was the chef for making the haupia, and Uncle Willie and my brother Sonny, my sister Judy and I helping with the preparation of the raw crab, lomi lomi salmon, chicken luau, dried squid and dried aku.

The day prior to the luau, several Uncles, Keli'i and Sonny with Uncle Willie in charge re-shaped the imu to fit the keawe wood and rocks design.

Early the morning of the luau, they lit the fire; and two hours later began the real work of placing the heated rocks into slits made in the pigs containing salt and shoyu rubbed in by Uncle Willie, closing the chicken wire around the pigs and lowering them onto the heated rocks, then placing banana stumps and leaves over the encased pigs, followed by water-soaked potato sacks, then canvas that covered the entire imu and finally the shoveling of dirt around the edges of the canvas to ensure no smoke escaped.

Approximately 6-8 hours later the imu-opening ceremony began.

The day of and the day after the luau were events that shaped my life...incredible tasting food gathered and prepared by each of us in the truest sense of a native Hawaiian luau where members of a family did everything together; of music played and sung by all; of shared laughter and merriment; and even of freely flowing beer and the after effects.

But it was the symbolic passage into manhood that I remember, to be accepted by my Uncles, older cousins and brother into their circle, to be regarded as an adept student of native Hawaiian traditions.

Over the many years that I would stop by to visit Aunty Ka'akau and Uncle Willie, who by the way were my Mother's favorite family members, Aunty always greeted me with great warmth, kind words and genuine Aloha, even until the evening that, as Kathy and I had just said hello to her, she at age 94 departed minutes later and went to join Uncle Willie.

Aunty's obituary noted she passed away on 9 August 1997 at her home in Waikane, observing that she was:

> "Born in Waikane, Koolaupoko, survived by children Joann Mersberg, Mary Aipia, Lily Galderia and Hattie Lederer; and hanai children McRonald K. Kamaka, Kevin K, Aipia and Judy M.P. Tsutsui."

I believe that all four women – Joann, Mary, Lily and Hattie – were Uncle Willie's and Mary Pahia's daughters. Thus, Uncle Willie Pahia had been previously married prior to marrying Aunty Ka'akau, she, however, for the first time.

I have no recollection of the four daughters, except for Aunty Mary Aipia who, along with Uncle Charlie Aipia and their two daughters and one son, lived next door to Uncle Willie and Aunty Ka'akau.

Big Aunty and Uncle Willie were the truest of native Hawaiians, who lived, spoke and practiced the values of native Hawaiians; we will never see the likes of them again – ever.

They are buried side by side with my sister, Judy Mae Puahaunani, who chose to rest with her *hanai* parents, a lasting tribute to the love and respect they shared among each other but no less than the love Judy Mae had for our parents, Bob and Lucy.

Chapter 6.   William Keliiahonui Kamaka, 1905 – 2004

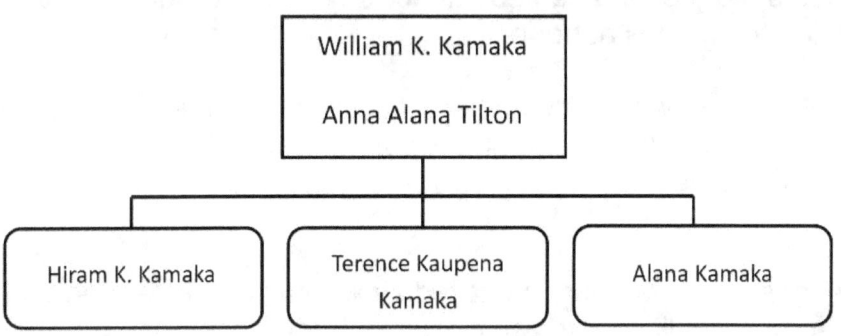

Uncle Willie Kamaka, born in 1905 and died in 1985, was the tallest of all my Uncles, standing at least 6'4", fit and thin in stature but with a striking toughness in the way he carried himself and walked.

As the fourth child born to my Grandparents, he always seemed erudite and interesting as we engaged in a number of conversations, most of which he initiated.

But there seemingly was a curtain drawn between Uncle Willie and the rest of the Kamaka family, for seldom did he participate in the Saturday evening Kamaka family meetings at my parents' home and seldom was he present in and around the Kamaka property.

Some of his absence may have been attributable to his devotion to his wife, Aunty Anna Alana Tilton, who, born in 1906 and died in 1987, had been married earlier to a Morita. She was a single-minded lady who knew where she was going and how to get there. Aunty Anna exuded a non-nonsense approach to relationships, not tolerating less than one's full commitment to any undertaking.

Aunty Anna and my Mother struck up a warm relationship in the late 1950's and beyond, based on their affinity for playing cards, more specifically the game of Paiute, a quasi-gambling card game that resembles poker but not a traditionally wagering game.

They were joined by Aunty Rachel and Aunty Annie, but it seems that my Mother was the ring leader of the group who not only encouraged the card games but actively pursued Aunty Anna hosting the games at her home.

My Mother knew that my Father would not have tolerated the card games being held at our home; so she drummed up the recreational aspects of card playing that eventually worked its way into gambling at prices they could afford.

I never saw my Mother so excited as when it was time, normally mid-day, to walk over to Aunty Anna's home.

Once or twice I walked over to Aunty Anna's to see my Mother, but somehow Uncle Willie intercepted me as we chatted about things in general; in short, I only recall entering Aunty Anna's home once, and it was well organized and appointed, much as she was.

Uncle and Aunty adopted a son, Hiram, born in 1927 and died in 2004 at the age of 76, who graduated from St. Louis High School, Creighton University, Creighton Law School and accepted into the practice of law in the State of Hawaii in 1954.

Hiram entered the Hawaii political arena as a Democrat, and almost immediately upon graduating from law school, volunteered to work for George Ariyoshi's first campaign for the territorial House of Representative.

Hiram was elected four times, 1958 -1968, representing the 8th District as a Representative to the State House of Representatives; appointed in 1968 as Governor John Burns' Budget Director; announced his candidacy and ran for Mayor of the City and County of Honolulu in 1980 but lost simply because he did not have the financial resources; and appointed in 1986 as the Director of Parks and Recreation.

Hiram ended his public service as the Budget Director for the City and County of Honolulu.

Hiram was also a talented musician, an engaging Native Hawaiian but quietly kept his distance from the Kamaka family. It was not unusual for Hiram to be at his parents' home and not be seen roaming about visiting the Kamaka cousins or his Aunts and Uncles.

The very few times we chatted were during my university days; I knew Hiram was very competent in anything he did, a good cousin and a low key Native Hawaiian; at one occasion he offered to send me to Creighton Law School if I were so inclined, but I was not.

Between 1994 and 2017, I traveled nearly monthly between Hawaii and Old Town, Alexandria, and always heard of Hiram through colleagues, especially those who played tennis as Hiram had become a fixture at Diamond Head Tennis Courts, a public court at the south end of Waikiki and apparently a very competent doubles player.

I joined my sister Judy and her husband, Muts, and my brother Sonny and his wife, Elizabeth, to say farewell to Hiram at his morning memorial service at Star of the Sea Catholic Church; Hiram's brother and sister, Terence Kaupena Kamaka and Alana Kamaka, were hosting the memorial service; and as we exchanged hugs and greetings with each of them,

I mentioned to my brother that while I remember Kaupena visiting Aunty Anna and Uncle Willie, I had no recollection of Alana, though my sister Judy had maintained consistent contact with both of them.

Chapter 7.   Joseph K. Kamaka, 1906 – 1978

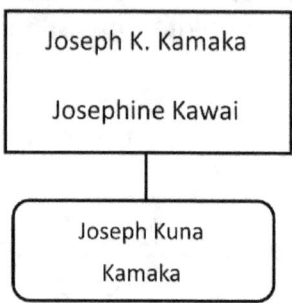

Uncle Joe and Aunty Josephine Kawai lived among the Kamaka family brothers and sisters but primarily kept to themselves.

Their home was built on a hillside that sloped to the ocean so that you entered their home at the top of the hill but the construction left a large airy space between the home's one level floor and the ground, sort of like being held up by stilts but with more formidable 2x4's.

The built their home along the shoreline, planted coconut trees, kept the grass mowed every week and their property was used by all of us as the departure point as we waded into deep water to swim.

Judy, Miguel (Son) and I would often visit Aunty Josephine during lunch time for she would make us sandwiches or provide cookies; and I recall falling asleep on their living room floor on more than one occasion.

They allowed us to wander through the yard but seldom did we meander to the back side of their home to see the vegetable gardens and pigs that Uncle Joe nurtured.

He was not an inviting nor socially warm person; frankly most of my Uncles were quiet, hard- working and thoughtful men who spoke only when they had to.

Uncle Joe and Aunty Josephine adopted a son, Joseph Kuna, several years younger than I, who graduated from Castle High School, got married, joined the Hawaii Army National Guard and one day became the focus of a manhunt by the Oahu Police. Arrested, tried and convicted, he died of cancer during his imprisonment in the Halawa Correctional Facility, or Halawa Penitentiary, Honolulu.

My vivid recollection of Uncle Joe was not of him, necessarily, but of his black, knee length rubber boots that he wore everywhere he went; he was mated to his black, knee length rubber boots.

Chapter 8.   Ronald K. Kamaka, 1907 - 1980

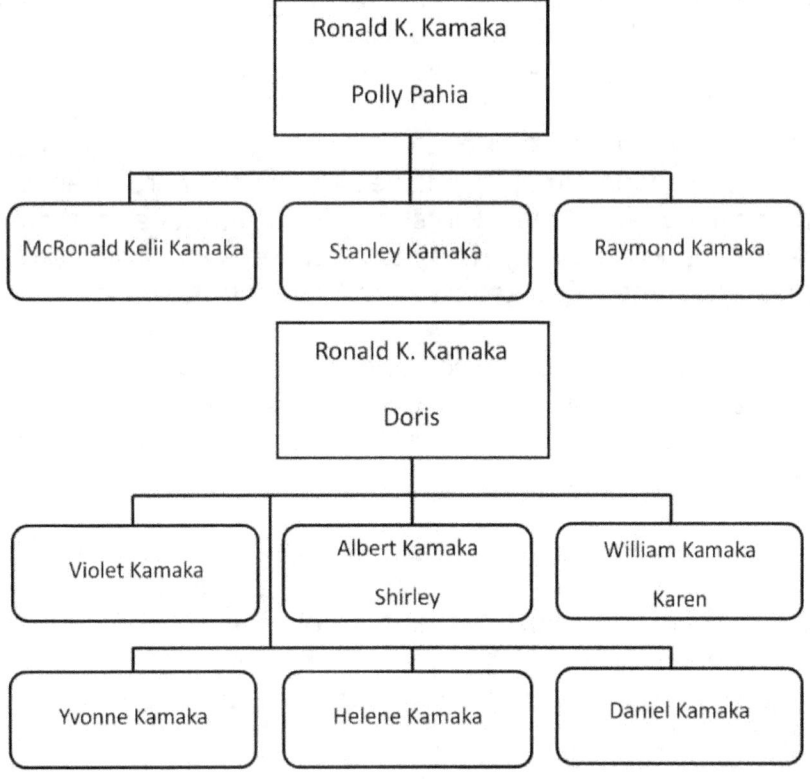

Uncle Ronald and his first wife had three sons - McRonald, Stanley and Raymond, all of whom were introduced earlier. I don't recall his first wife, Polly Pahia, who was the daughter of Uncle Willie Pahia, though I can only surmise that she had passed away from the complications of an illness.

Uncle Ronald then married Aunty Doris, and they had six children, Violet, Albert Alapake, William Kahiwa, Yvonne, Helene and Daniel who passed away in December 2016.

Uncle Ronald was a direct man who always seemed to be on edge, at least it appeared so as he seemed to challenge nearly every issue impacting the Kamaka family; he appeared to welcome advocating the other side of a position, oftentimes with a great deal of objectivity and common sense.

It was his argumentative approach, however, that made him appear on edge, somewhat of an attacking warrior, but one who did not abide by Roberts Rules of Order or a structured process with some protocols; the process did not matter.

I recall returning home after a late Saturday night to a Kamaka family meeting wherein all my Uncles and Aunts were freely and openly arguing, oftentimes with strong vigor, further apportionment of the land on which Aunty Ka'akau lived, the surrounding areas, and the 187 acres in Waikane Valley, among other things.

I sat in the patio listening to the various points of view and was just amazed at Uncle Ronald's incisiveness compared to my other Uncles who said little or to my Father who, as the host, matched Uncle Ronald's discourse.

As I often mentioned to my Mother after weeks of listening to the Saturday evenings' Kamaka family gatherings at our home, that if all Native Hawaiians were like the Native Hawaiians of the Kamaka family, then very, very little progress for the future of Native Hawaiians, resolved by Native Hawaiians, would be made.

The numerous Kamaka family gatherings on Saturday evenings at our Waikane home displayed the character of my Aunts and Uncles, their willingness to speak with their soul, their attentiveness to the issues, and their unrelenting attitude that it is better to keep the oratory alive than it is to achieve a consensus agreement.

Their meetings would have been a substantive, original research project for a psychologist or sociologist; the study's results may have, perhaps would have, predicted quite accurately the struggles today of our Native Hawaiians; while the environment certainly plays the hand that is dealt, it is the DNA that deals the hand.

My five male first cousins – Keli'i, Stanley, Raymond, Albert and William – were Waikane's athletic dynamos.

Each was a starter for Castle High School's football team, and I believe all five were selected to the Honolulu Advertiser's First Team of their league with Keli'i as a lineman; Stanley as a tight end; Raymond as a wide receiver; Albert as a running back; and William as a wide receiver.

Each went in different directions after high school.

Keli'i became a famous professional wrestler with championship belts; Stanley became the father of one of our State's gifted athletes; Raymond won a scholarship to play collegiate football but ended his days a passionate advocate for Native Hawaiian rights.

Albert, now retired from the Kaneohe Fire Department, continues Raymond's advocacy but within the Kamaka family.

William, who spent nearly two years at the Church College of Hawaii, Laie, Oahu (now known as Brigham Young University, Hawaii), married Karen, died as a young man with four children, a death that came too soon and reverberates to this day that a person, as pleasant and wonderful as William, can be taken well before his time.

All five were inquisitive regarding issues and eager for knowledge but none more so than Keli'i and Raymond, the former working within the rules and the latter challenging the rules.

They were the Ying and the Yang, the two sides of their father, Uncle Ronald, but no one possessed the Aloha spirit, the graciousness of the soul of Native Hawaiians more so than William; he was more like Uncle John, Aunty Ka'akau, Aunty Rachel and my Mother rolled into one.

When my family and I were at the United States Military Academy at West Point, 1974-1977, during my tenure as an Assistant Professor of English, Keli'i was then a rising star in the world of professional wrestling under the name of Dr. Moto.

It was during Thanksgiving 1976, a cold, snowy day that Keli'i drove up to West Point to join Kathy and me as guests of the Cadets from Hawaii for the traditional Thursday Thanksgiving Dinner in the Cadet Dining Hall.

Keli'i pulled up to our home at West Point about 5:00 pm, stepped out of his car dressed in a white suit, wearing a white Panama, toquilla constructed hat, and a goatee on his chin.

Against the darkened sky, the grayness of the ground, his natural dark brown skin wrapped around 350 pounds of muscle, Keli'i looked like a demon rising from the swirling mist coming to bellow out our missteps. Then he was at our door, warmly hugging Troy, Brad and Ethan, Kathy and me.

Thanksgiving Dinner at the Cadet Dining Hall is a formal event; with Kathy resplendent in her dinner outfit and I in my Dress Blues, we drove to a parking space along the Library and walked over to the massive Cadet Dining Hall where several dozens of the invited guests had already gathered.

I signaled to Kathy and Keli'i to allow most of the invited guest to walk up the steps and enter the Cadet Dining Hall before we started our ascent.

We were the last to enter the Cadet Dining Hall, and the first table we encountered was Lieutenant General Sid Berry's table surrounded by his family and guests.

Picture a Lieutenant Colonel in Dress Blues, his five foot wife resplendent in her evening attire, and following a step to our left is Keli'i in his all-white suit with white Panama hat on his shaven head; we were not prepared for what followed.

Lieutenant General Berry, the Superintendent of USMA, suddenly stepped away from his chair, reached out to greet and shake Keli'i's hand, and mentioned that he was a huge fan of his and was looking forward to the coming Saturday evening's individual wrestling championship match at Madison Square Garden between Bruno Samarrtino, the current individual wrestling champion who had held the championship belt twice for a total of 11 years, and the challenger, my cousin Keli'i, aka Dr. Moto.

Kathy and I were dazed as we broke free and escorted Keli'i to the table with the Cadets from Hawaii.

But more was to come.

There were more than 100 waiters who lined the wall waiting after the grace was said to enter the kitchen to bring out the food items; nearly 1/3 of the wait staff, rather than bringing out the food items, rushed to our table and asked Keli'i to autograph the Thanksgiving menus.

He started to jot down inscriptions in Kanji, the logographic Chinese characters that are used in modern Japanese writing, and mumbled something in Japanese to the lined-group of waiters until their Supervisor came by and asked:

"Dr. Moto" would you be willing to sign the menus after dinner?"

Keli'i concurred.

The Supervisor then ushered the waiters back to their duties; the Thanksgiving Dinner was served, though waiters kept coming back throughout the dinner to ask Keli'i for his autograph; and he was the only one of the thousands of Cadets and guests who went without a Thanksgiving dinner that evening.

The Hawaii Cadets were ecstatic with pride and Aloha; Keli'i was overwhelmed by meeting the Superintendent, a fan, and the reception by all; the wait staff was overjoyed at their good fortune; the Corps of Cadet was treated to an honored sports figure.

Kathy and I were simply amazed that a boy from Waikane grew to become a national sports celebrity, enthusiastically welcomed in the Halls from which our Nation's military leaders and Presidents of our great country were educated.

And I jotted down in my memory bank an unforgettable evening with my first cousin with whom I had shared youthful, fond experiences with our sister, Judy Mae Puahaunani, in Waikane.

Events that illuminate life must be recorded.

Keli'i was, as Lee Cataluna wrote in August 2007, "a villain fans loved to hate."

Lee's article summarizes his incredible journey from a *hanai* son to a world and national sports hero; Keli'i made a difference with his life, in spite of the twists and turns of a world that did much to marginalize minorities.

He rose off the mat time and time again, promising his fans and ring side announcers the riches of the Orient only to respond later when asked to produce these goods, "No chancee," reinforcing the good-guy-turned-bad image.

He understood human psychology but respected any who cheered for or against him.

In the summer of 1968 my Mother visited Kathy, the three boys and me at Fort Knox, Kentucky during my 10-month class at the Armor Advance Course.

Invited by Keli'i and his first wife, Karen, to spend the weekend with them and attend his Saturday evening World Tag Team match against the Bruiser and the Crusher in Indianapolis, Indiana, we packed up the boys and six of us drove in our little 1500 VW to their apartment in Indianapolis.

My Mother opted out attending Keli'i's match, stayed in the apartment to baby sit the boys while Kathy and Karen drove to the match.

Keli'i and I rode in his Cadillac an hour earlier but parked nearly a mile away from the auditorium in a somewhat secluded location; he reached into his trunk and pulled out the massive World Tag Team trophy which he carried as we walked to the auditorium.

Along the way, a long line of cars were moving slowly to the parking lot of the auditorium, and the verbal abuse heaped on Keli'i was unlike anything I had ever heard.

I suddenly realized why the torrent of verbal abuse.

Throughout the day of the match, the TV sports and news channels had been playing over and over the marketing pitch during which Keli'i spoke in broken Japanese with the TV camera hovering over his massive back with a silhouette of his face.

Keli'i spoke these words,

> "You Americans all stupid; we bomb you; we destroy you; and now I am champion; *bakatare* (idiotic) Americans."

It was a miracle that groups of fans did not rush from their cars to assault us.

As Keli'i and his partner, Mitsu Arakawa, wearing wooden geta sandals to reinforce their Oriental image approached the ring and

Keli'i mounted the steps to enter the ring, an elderly lady rushed to the steps and pounded his foot with a heavy iron lamp which drew a huge ovation from the more than 10,000 customers.

The Bruiser and The Crusher, white professional wrestlers, won the first fall by pinning Arakawa. They were close to winning the deciding second fall until Keli'i judo-chopped the Bruiser with such force that the Bruiser actually flipped over on the mat and was then pinned by Keli'i.

Sitting at ring side, I stood up and cheered my cousin.

After several seconds, I noticed I was the only one in the entire auditorium standing, as Kathy or Karen thought better.

Those around me just starred with disbelief that in heartland America, just 23 years removed from WW II, anyone would publicly dare to support the hated Japanese wrestlers....Dr. Moto and Arakawa.

Then a young lad, encouraged by his Dad, approached me and asked if I could get Dr. Moto to sign his program.

Then I knew that someone in the future would describe Keli'i as "a villain fans loved to hate."

During the third fall sequence, The Bruiser and The Crusher threw both Keli'i and Arakawa out of the ring which led to many ringside customers using their metal chairs to pound Keli'i and assuage their frustrations.

I quietly led Kathy and Karen out of the auditorium during the melee, concerned for our lives.

A few years ago Muts invited me to a meeting with Raymond and Stanley, who now lives in a modern apartment complex built in Waimanalo and leased by the Department of Hawaiian Homelands to qualified Native Hawaiians, to meet and listen to a trio of advocates on Native Hawaiian land rights.

The storyline by the trio was fascinating, nearly compelling, but the substance of the facts and evidence was rooted in myths, legends and third party interpretations.

Stanley and Raymond were reassured by the advocates that they, Stanley and Raymond, indeed owned all the land that is now Waiahole, Waikane, Hakipu'u, Kuloa and Ka'a'awa; that Raymond's recent legal filing with the State of Hawaii Land Commission by itself proved his legal ownership; and that Raymond, as Ali'i Nui of all the inherited land just mentioned, could dispense with the land as he saw proper.

Muts, who sat at the small dining table throughout the recitation, feigned interest; and I was left to acclaim:

"That is remarkable."

At the conclusion of the 2-hour session, Raymond confided to Muts and me that he was having land ownership issues with his younger brother which echoed for me the Saturday evening meetings of challenges and arguments many years ago among the Kamaka family at our home in Waikane.

But as we parted that morning, I left happy as I got to meet Stanley and Raymond once again; happy that Muts was able to arrange the meeting at Stanley's apartment, but somewhat sad that my first cousins were convinced that right was on their side and were looking forward to apportioning all that land from Waiahole, Waikane, Hakipu'u, Kuloa and Ka'a'awa.

We all walked away rather satisfied that we knew what was applicable.

Raymond and I saw each other early one morning in 2014 as I was walking to the Hui's office on Bishop Street; Raymond was sitting as a passenger in a rather beaten up vehicle that somehow escaped any Vehicle Safety Inspection for the past few years.

As they drove slowly by me on Queen Street, he called out:

"Cuz, Aloha."

I responded:

"Hui, pehea oe."

I never saw him again; he passed away in May 2014, a sad day for the Kamaka family.

Aunty Doris and her eldest daughter, Violet, died in an automobile crash on the Pali Highway as they returned home early one morning from work at the Pineapple Cannery in Honolulu; their deaths devastated the entire Kamaka family.

Violet was not only an energetic young lady but also a generous person who looked like her brother, Albert; while we lived just meters from each other, Violet and I only exchanged greetings whenever I returned home from Kamehameha's campus.

Yvonne, or Lehua, was physically more like William, or Kahiwa; both were striking in stature and appearance, blessed with a warmth that immediately transferred itself to others. Lehua moved to the mainland sometime after her mother's accident, seldom, if ever, returning to Waikane.

Daniel, the youngest son, recently passed away at age 56 on December 2016. I never knew him as we were a generation apart.

Chapter 9.   Aunty Annie Amelia Kamaka, 1910 – 1993

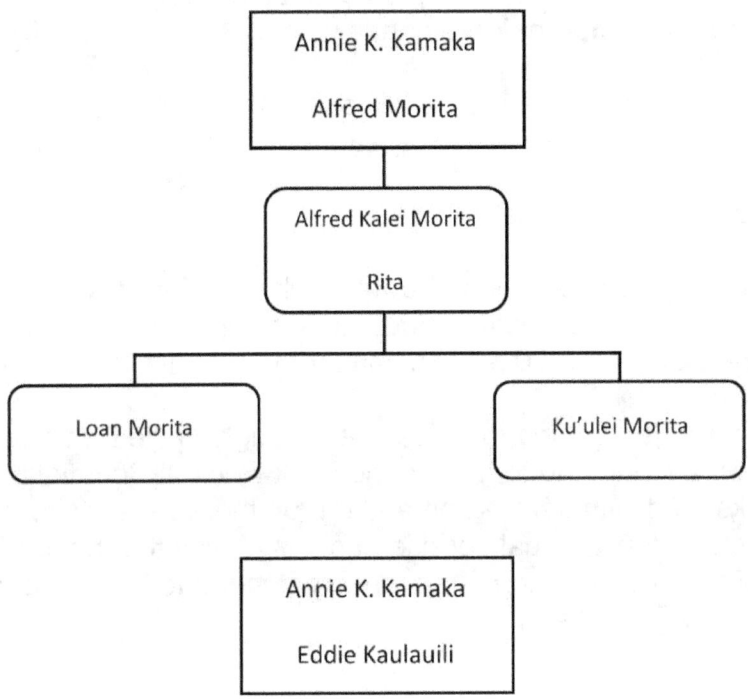

Aunty Annie, born in 1910 and died in 1993, was the prettiest Kamaka daughter, second only to my Mother, who enjoyed life's activities, was quick to smile and laugh, self-assured, confident and orchestrated a willingness to engaged in small talk story, medium talk story and large talk story.

She was the flower that never grew tired nor wilted nor withered; she was the precise opposite of Aunty Kaakau, Aunty Thelma, Aunty Rachel, and somewhat like my Mother but more outgoing, assertive.

Married to Alfred Morita who together raised their son, my eldest cousin, Alfred Kalei Morita, Aunty Annie became attached in later years to my eldest sister, Betty Lou, or Betty Lou found a second mother in Aunty Annie which was not unusual in Native Hawaiian families of that time.

Aunty Annie and Aunty Anna both married a Morita, and both apparently divorced their Morita husbands or they were widows. It is unknown whether their husbands were of the same family.

Eventually Aunty Annie married Eddie Kalauli, a Non-Commissioned Officer Staff Sergeant E-6 who had served in the Korean War with the 27th Infantry Regiment, The Wolfhounds, and was stationed at Schofield Barracks.

Uncle Eddie drove a Green, 4-door, stick shift Ford sedan to Schofield Barracks, leaving about 3:00 am and returning to Waikane well after 6:00 pm the same day.

Their marriage seemed to thrive even though Uncle Eddie spent most of his waking hours during the work week at Schofield Barracks; and with Leroy, Son and me on the weekends teaching us how to shoot a 22-caliber rifle at glass bottles that hung on the patio of the deserted home that once belonged to Uncle Ronald (Karen now lives there).

We fired at the hanging bottles, generally missed, as the bullets whizzed out into the ocean; but Uncle Eddie never seemed to miss, regardless of the position he took…sitting, kneeling or prone.

It was this activity that rallied my first cousins and me to Uncle Eddie, as we were the first to greet him as he returned home from Schofield Barracks and spent time talking story when he had the day off.

Apparently at work one day he had an altercation with and struck a Lieutenant; I can only guess that he was offered a court-martial or resignation, and he decided that he and the United States Army were no longer in cadence, that it was time for him to return to civilian life.

Early one morning, he drove away; he left Waikane, never to return.

After several days of his absence, I mentioned to my Mother that I had not seen Uncle Eddie; and that is the point at which my Mother related what she knew.

Aunty Annie was home-bound for several days, not venturing out of her home until my Mother encouraged her to walk in the sunshine because worries seem to take on a different perspective when measured in daylight.

The last I saw of Uncle Eddie Kalauli, Aunty Annie's second husband, was his driving an Emergency Medical Ambulance as I pulled my Studebaker off to the side as he raced past me with lights flashing.

Kalei, Aunty Annie's only child, was highly intelligent, assertive, outgoing and loved playing the guitar or riding his Harley Davidson motorcycle which he employed well and benefitted from as he courted the beautiful Rita, who loved to ride the back seat of Kalei's motorcycle, until she accepted his proposal of marriage.

They raised two wonderful daughters, Lona and Ku'ulei, my second cousins, who grew up with all of us in Waikane; somewhat younger than I, they spent a lot of time at Aunty Rachel's home just visiting as Aunty Rachel's daughters, Manu, Harriet and Carol, were about their age.

Lona and my sister Judy Mae became close allies in later years, and I always had a warm spot for Lona and Ku'ulei.

During my sophomore year at the University, I caught a ride every morning with Kalei and Rita to a drop off point close to the University.

The morning rides were full of exceptional dialogue between Kalei and Rita that only a back seat rider could enjoy – biting, unrestrained claims and counterclaims about finances, living conditions, raising Lona and Ku'ulei, dealing with the Kamaka family, yardwork, overscheduling the weekends – it was a miracle that they stopped short of actually hitting each other.

The drop off point did not come soon enough, though I enjoyed the give-and-take arguments, especially in Kalei's relatively new light colored, 4-door Cadillac that he absolutely loved.

Rita often would be quiet for a 10-15 minute stretch, but that was because she was applying her makeup; shortly thereafter, the arguments would begin in earnest once again.

Rita was strikingly beautiful but there was a side to her that conveyed an unsettled spirit, a less than happy attitude that every now and then surfaced; I suspect much of my outlook derived from the early morning rides to the drop off point, though I seldom thought Kalei was anything but noble.

Yet, there were many occasions when Rita and I greeted each other with warmth and sincerity. It wasn't until we were much older that our respect for each other surfaced.

But their two daughters, Lona and Ku'ulei, were especially special to me.

Two of the many Kalei-stories involved his love of playing the guitar claiming to having found the "lost key" in slack key music, a cord which he played for me several times; and his consumption of beer in his later years; he reminded me of my Uncle Abraham who was a happy beer drinker.

In her later years, Aunty Annie became a caring and compassionate sounding board, a good listener to the growing pains of my sister, Betty Lou, as she embarked on being a mother, wife, business executive and manager of two businesses, Hardwoods Hawaii and Garments Hawaii.

They shared private moments, cried on each other's shoulders, arrived at solutions for difficult problems, and became a symbolic mother and daughter.

On one occasion, my sister shared with me Aunty Annie's decision to leave her principal Waikane home to my sister; I objected; and so did my younger sister, Judy Mae; and my sister, Betty Lou, eventually declined Aunty Annie's gift.

The future, had Betty Lou persisted, would have been darkened forever.

Aunty Annie passed away in 1993; she has been missed.

Chapter 10. Aunty Thelma Kekinookalani Kamaka, 1912 - 1963

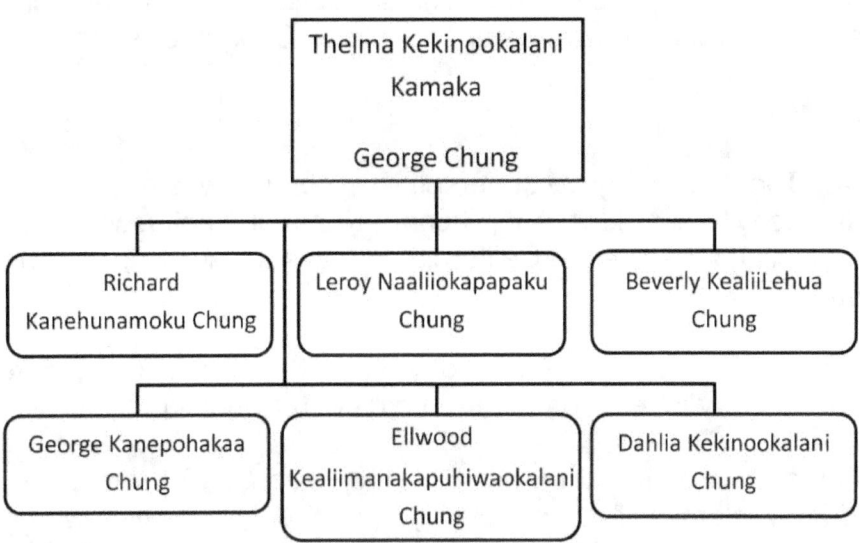

Aunty Thelma and her husband, Uncle George, raised four sons and two girls initially at 321 North Kuakini Street, the Kamaka home in Honolulu that is now part of the parking lot of Kuakini Hospital, before they drew the lot in Waikane on which they built their home.

Aunty Thelma was an extraordinary lady who exuded a genuine spirit of Aloha to everyone; she never met a stranger she did not know.

Her home became the gathering place for all the 27 Kamaka cousins; the sleeping floor for some of us; the home for meals for nearly all of us, and the location for Kelii to play the piano, for Dukie to play the ukulele, and for Kalei to strum his guitar.

Aunty Thelma provided the comfort we 27 cousins required, the home for family visitors, and she did it so flawlessly and easily.

Yet she was never at ease.

She lost her husband, Uncle George, in the summer of 1950. I remember it well.

Aunty Thelma was devastated; she sat outside the back door in the open garage all night waiting for Uncle George to return.

He never did.

Aunty Thelma, who gave of herself to everyone, was not so fortunate with her eldest son, Richard Kanehunamoku, who left for the mainland, traveled to California and was not seen again, and he has since died.

Aunty and I discussed the next day an incident that occurred after I returned early in the morning from a date in Honolulu.

As I made the turn 300 meters from the Waiahole Poi Factory, I suddenly felt myself actually falling asleep, only to somehow grip the steering wheel with such force that I missed crashing into the bridge 10 meters from the Waiahole Poi Factory.

Looking back in my rear view mirror, I saw what appeared to be a fiery red ball about a hundred meters trailing me.

Aunty offered that her son, Richard, suffered a severe car accident but a year ago at the same spot, and that he had described the same fiery red ball a second before his accident.

I was lucky.

Leroy Naaliiokapapaku, the second son, was the inspiration for his two other brothers, Ellwood Kealiimanakapuhiwaokalani, and

George Kanepohakaa (nicknamed Juneboy); and sisters, Beverly Jean Kealiilehua and Dalhia Louise Kekinookalani.

Leroy was self-driven, focused, intelligent and hard-working; and he was always assertive in seeking and effectively using knowledge; an avid fisherman, much better than I, but not equal to our other cousin, Miguel (Son).

He courted Martha, whose father was a policeman, with vigor and a sense of purpose, marrying Martha and raising two daughters, both of whom are graduates of Kamehameha Schools while one is a practicing attorney.

And a son who has been working diligently to measure up to his parents' accomplishments.

Leroy, Son and I played football, softball and lifted weights throughout our teenage years, but Leroy was focused on his karate, training every day by striking the padded 1x4 pole, one of four, that supported the open garage; he began his freshman year at the University of Hawaii-Manoa, and even though he was doing well, dropped out as finances were difficult.

Lehua and Kekino were the sisters whose conduct, warmth and genuine laugher were exemplary. They reflected the grace of their mother, Aunty Thelma, but were not able to exhibit the same drive of their Father, Uncle George, or their brother, LeRoy, because of social policies of the time.

Yet both were attractive girls who became beautiful ladies, married well and have been superb mothers.

George, or Juneboy, challenged his brother LeRoy at every turn; energetic, spirited and self-determined, Juneboy established himself as an entrepreneur by taking on a job as a one-person luggage handler and ticket taker at Kaunakakai Airport on the Island of Molokai.

In those days, 1960's, Kaunakakai Airport, Molokai, saw one plane arrive and take off a day.

But when I went to Molokai in 1997, Juneboy had been promoted to Airport Manager many years ago with the responsibility for the funding and operational standards of the entire, modern Kaunakakai Airport which now saw a multitude of take offs and arrivals every day of the week.

He also earned the reputation on Molokai as an expert fisherman and a hard working Native Hawaiian; and that of itself is unique as Moloka'i Native Hawaiians seldom offer accolades; one has to earn his accomplishments to receive their kudos.

When I arrived at Kaunakakai one day on Pacific American Foundation business, we visited, talked story and recalled the Waikane days of our youth.

Upon my departure from Molokai later that day, I felt a huge surge of pride that a Kamaka had made his way, successfully, in life's many turns.

Ellwood was always born to Waikane; an incredibly special person, he always greeted each day with such a positive attitude that it draped over you.

He started his own limousine driving business, among other things, and offered his services to me on one occasion; Ellwood was much like his mother in every way, generous, warm and totally loyal to the Kamaka family.

I never heard him say an unkind remark about anyone.

Aunty Thelma probably had a more difficult life than her sisters, but remarkable that she opened her home to all of us. She was the modern caregiver to the many nephews and nieces who required a good and sensitive listener.

She never said a harsh word to any of us.

But her children were her blessing; they were and are phenomenal human beings.

Chapter 11. Lucy Kapaeloa Kamaka, 1913 – 1974

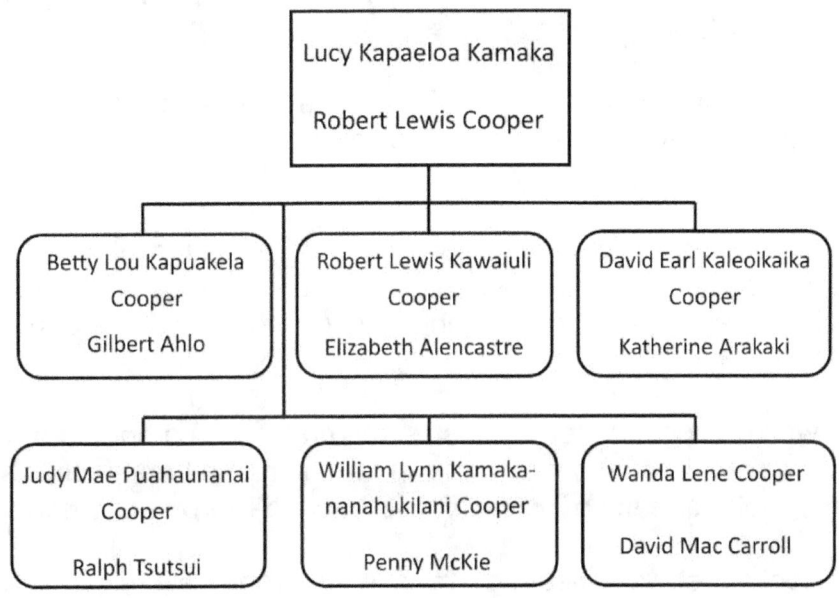

I offer my apologies to the readers at the start of this chapter, for it will be a lengthy recollection of memories of my parents, sister, brothers and their children. This is the part of the narrative that is nonfiction, at least I trust it will be.

In early February 2017, I submitted my DNA sample for official testing to the Ancestry DNA association; after several weeks, they sent me an email with the results which are recorded below:

48% Polynesia (Native Hawaiian)

46% Europe

- 18% Ireland

- 14% Great Britain

- 6% Scandinavian

- 5% Iberian Peninsula

- 2% Europe West

- <1% Finland/NW Russia

The results conform to our understanding of our genealogy, passed down to us principally by my Mother and defended by my sister, Judy Mae.

While Judy Mae was still alive, she and I argued about our native Hawaiian percentage; now we have scientific evidence buttressed by a high degree of validity.

Our Mother was uniquely extraordinary and gifted lady who foresaw the importance of education and consistency of effort to reach a level of success that could allow us to reach back and help others.

She worked continuously to ensure the house was a home for all of us, waking at 4:00 am every morning to ensure breakfast was on the table for each of us before we headed to work, or wherever.

She cooked, sewed, cleaned, washed and ironed every piece of clothing, using the iron roller or a flat iron with an ironing board.

She prepared three meals a day for us, including three staples at every dinner…potatoes for my Father, rice and poi for us.

She magically kept all six of us calm, assigning scheduled dinner duties posted to a kitchen cabinet door, and clipped the hair from around our ears and neck fashioned to a style that she thought was flattering and appropriate.

There wasn't anything my Mother would not do for the six of us. She was omniscient and omnipotent, not godly, but like all mothers everywhere, unstoppable.

She learned the medicinal healing power of indigenous plants, like crushing the hibiscus petals into a soft paste which healed boils and skin infections, as she did for Wanda.

In her later years, she pledged, as legal collateral, her land assets of Waikane Valley and the property on which our home sat for the purchases of Hardwoods Hawaii and Garments Hawaii.

My Mother and Father worked long hours during their retirement years at both locations, providing not only expert wood carving skills (my Father) but also sustaining the people relationships (my Mother) that determine the levels of success of any business.

Both my parents were admired by the wholesalers, marketing developers, customers and employees, but my Mother was truly loved by all.

She was the quintessential business executive, intelligent, kind, thoughtful, focused, multitasker, insightful communications skills, and a deeply sensitive leader.

But there was the *maka'ainana* (common citizen) side of my Mother; she would sit on the patio steps and ask me to tweezer the white strands of hair that was showing up; and I dutifully complied, but only for 10-15 minutes at which time I declared, "That's it, Mom; all the white hair have been pulled."

She knew better, and turned to Judy or Wanda and asked that they continue where I left off. And they dutifully complied.

My Mother loved the gospel singing of Mahalia Jackson, but she kept Mahalia's album in a secret location.

One day I saw the corner of the album tucked away in her clothes closet, pulled it down, and asked my Mother about the album and why she kept it hidden.

She looked at me rather exasperated, took the album and placed it back in its proper place.

I realized why she reacted so differently, as music held such an important place in our Native Hawaiian culture. And the gospel music of Mahalia Jackson had a special place in her heart.

We were hapa children, half white and half Native Hawaiian; being raised in Hawaii, we did not make a distinction among anyone, let alone our cousins, classmates and friends.

My parents had never said a word about different races; they treated everyone with respect and expected all of us to do the same; I admire our parents who, in spite of social values of their time, married for love; though he was the first haole in the Kamaka family, they never looked back at their decision.

But it was not until years later did I begin to understand the culture of racism in our country.

My first real experience with racist attitudes came somewhat innocently.

My first assignment as a Second Lieutenant was to the 1st Battalion, 7th Infantry Regiment, "Cottonbalers," in Aschaffenburg, West Germany, a town on the outskirts of the spessarts (range of low wooded mountains) and an hour's drive from Frankfurt.

I reported to the Battalion during the winter of January 1964; and with my host officer, arrived for my scheduled morning interview with the Battalion Commander, Lieutenant Colonel Jesse J. Atkins.

After the normal formalities, Lieutenant Colonel Akins remarked that he had served with Captain Kenneth Good who had been killed in action in Vietnam in 1963, and Lieutenant Colonel Atkins knew that I was one of Captain Good's pallbearers as he had been a ROTC Instructor at the University of Hawaii prior to being assigned to Vietnam as an Advisor to a South Vietnamese combat unit.

About that time Captain Barry Winkleman, an Army aviator and my first Company Commander, joined us.

Lieutenant Colonel Atkins then described his recent decision, already carried out, to place all soldiers of the Battalion awaiting Courts Martial in one company and then in one platoon, a centralization of sorts for the apparent efficiency of control and minimum operational disturbances.

The company was Company B; the Company Commander was Captain Winkleman; and the platoon was the 2nd Platoon.

And Lieutenant Colonel Atkins had recommended, and Captain Winkleman had concurred, that I was to be assigned as the Platoon Leader of the 2nd Platoon.

I walked with Captain Winkleman to meet my Platoon Sergeant, who was African American, who then introduced me to the entire platoon of 24 soldiers, all of whom were African Americans and twenty-two of whom had been charged with infractions of the Uniform Code of Military Justice.

They were the pariahs of the 1st Battalion, 7th Infantry Regiment, and I, who until that day had never seen an African American, was the leader of 24 African American soldiers who looked no different, generally, than my Kamaka uncles and male cousins.

I felt at home.

With this assignment, it helped me understand, but not appreciate, the ignorance of a Sears and Roebuck salesman in Kentucky and other incidents that reeked of crude and vulgar racism.

During my 10-month Armor Advanced Course in 1968 at Fort Knox, Kentucky, my Mother spent two weeks with us that I shall always remember.

She arrived at the Louisville Airport with a suitcase of gifts of Aloha shirts and muumuus for a few of my classmates who were ecstatic upon receiving the gifts; my Mother's philosophy of *makana* (gift) reflected her true Native Hawaiian spirit and traditions.

It was a hot and muggy summer; so shortly after her arrival, she suggested we go to the nearest Sears and Roebuck store to purchase a window air conditioner.

At the small retail store just outside of Fort Knox, the salesman rejected my Mother's Sears and Roebuck credit card as it was not a credit card issue by a Sears and Roebuck store in Kentucky.

The technicality was not lost on me; and neither my Mother nor we had thought to bring sufficient funds to purchase the window air conditioner.

As we negotiated with the salesman to find an equitable solution, I suddenly realized that we had come face to face with discrimination and racism. I, having just returned from the battlefields of Vietnam as an Infantry Company Commander, wanted to strike out at the salesman.

But my Mother and wife knew I was about to explode, and they calmly walked away with me in tow.

During the first summer (1972) of my studies for a Masters Degree in English Literature, Kathy's mother, Haruko, came for a visit from her residence in Lancaster, California.

She was responsible for our ability to make the down payment for the current home we purchased and lived in for two years before moving to our assignment to the Department of English, United States Military Academy, West Point, NY.

As she was getting ready to return to California, Kathy and I decided to go on a road trip with the boys and Haruko, driving the southern route from Kansas City to Lancaster; it was fun, enjoyable and a memorable time for all of us, except for the gas stop we made in Nevada during which time the service station attendant tried to sell us four (4) new tires for our 1970 metallic gray, four-door Monte Carlo Chevrolet.

We arrived in good order; spent a week in Lancaster visiting with Kathy's sister, Amy, and her husband, Dan, and their three children, Greg, Daniel and Ann; slept over at Haruko's apartment; completed a minor repair on my radiator that was overheating; spent time at the apartment complex's pool; and finally had to return back to our home in North Kansas City and my studies.

Also during my studies for a Masters Degree in English Literature at the University of Missouri-Kansas City, my Mother came for a two-week visit with the boys and us in during the summer of 1973 at the home we purchased at 7315 NW 73rd Terrace, North Kansas City, Missouri.

As usual, she brought the three boys all sort of gifts; enjoyed watching Troy and Brad play summer baseball in the local league; traveled with us to Sunday brunches at Red Roof Inn; rode in my yellow convertible MG Midget; and watched the evening TV programs until she was ready for bed.

It was so special having Haruko and now my Mother spending the last two summers with us.

The warm, muggy and humid weather contributed to my Mother's sudden fainting spells; and after a visit to the local clinic, the attending physician suggested that my Mother's heart medications were not the most effective nor appeared to be the latest cardiology medications, and that she was really quite ill.

I recall phoning my sisters to relay my concerns, and as it was time for my Mother to return to Hawaii, we drove her to the Kansas City International Airport, hugged each other, and said our Aloha.

Less than eight months later, my Mother died.

I flew home.

My Mother's memorial service lasted two days.

People from all walks of life passed by her casket, most unabashedly crying.

Uncle Ronald mentioned to me that when he sat at my Mother's bedside in the hospital during her final moments, tears flowed from her eyes.

But it was not until midday of the second day that the miracle happened.

There were no clouds in the sky; the morning was absolutely beautiful; the sun's rays broke over the Ko'olau mountains; and as we carried her casket from the front steps of the vestibule to place her on the carriage that was to carry her to her graveside, light showers fell just enough to dampen all of us.

We stopped in a moment of silence and awe. God, in His Heaven, joined by the Native Hawaiian gods of my Mother, blessed my Mother. *Kulu ka waimaka, uwe ka ʻopua* (The tears fall, the clouds weep). Born 26 September 1913, died 4 April 1974.

Our Father was unlike our Mother.

He was born with the Puritan work ethic in his blood, lived by it and ensured that Sonny and I followed in his footsteps.

He was not a difficult man to understand once you realized that he managed the six of us in groups of two…Sonny and I were the employee team; Betty Lou and Wanda were the Snow White pair; Judy rebelled at being manipulated and raced off to Aunty Kaʻakau; and Billy was pretty much on his own.

Our Father was a solid provider of things…home, cars, clothing, food, television, landscaping equipment…and understood the power of politics and relationships.

He rose from a common laborer to become the Superintendent of Maintenance, Public Schools, Department of Education.

During the early part of family requirements, he worked at two jobs, oftentimes taking me (at age 5-6) to his late night job in Honolulu of stripping the wax on the floors, then waxing and polishing office floors where I would hold the long electric cord as he buffed the floors. We would not be home until two or three o'clock in the morning.

An exacting worker, he was a most demanding and rigorous manager of public school grounds employees; on one occasion, I sat on his lap as he actually mowed the grass at Kahuku High School while the employees watched.

But, I must admit, I have many times spoken about how grass-cutting can be a much-admired avocation.

Keli'i, Raymond, Leroy, Son, and Juneboy were decidedly absent during the weekends, as they knew that my Father would round them up and give them work assignments if they were just walking around the Kamaka properties; they eventually discovered that white lies were generally accepted by my Father; such stretchers were actually funny, but my Father knew it was better to accept the stretchers rather than supervise them.

But there was the Irish side of him...humor, laughter, Sunday family cookouts where he was the Chef, gracious host to our friends that endeared him to all of us.

He loved to sit on his recliner to watch, at midnight Hawaii time, professional wrestling televised from Chicago; I still remember some of the wrestlers' names ...Lou Thez, Bruno Sammartino, Verne Gagne, Killer Kowalski, Andre the Giant.

I recall my Mother showing me a picture of my Father as a boxer during his service in the Army at Schofield Barracks; he was lean, muscled and rather handsome.

I suspect that my brothers and I inherited his DNA for athleticism.

And I know for sure that Betty Lou, Sonny, Judy Mae and I got some part of his competitiveness spirit.

My Father was fastidious in keeping his cars cleaned and polished; it seemed like a weekend ritual that we polished the car with a process...our Father put the wax on, Sonny was the lead wiper frequently turning over his cheese cloth; I followed with the second polishing cheese cloth, and Betty Lou had the final cheese cloth to ensure she wiped off any of the dried wax we may have missed.

Whenever Judy and Billy joined in, they were responsible for the hub caps and bumpers; but frankly they always seemed to be absent.

Since then, Sonny, Billy and I had become indoctrinated and programmed to drive and ride in clean, polished cars.

As parents, they had pretty clear cut duties and responsibilities; my Father was the hunter who brought things home; my Mother was the gatherer who placed things in their right locations to maximize their value.

Because all six of us boarded at Kamehameha Schools, our parents could never attend an athletic event or school function (Oratorical Contest) or class activity (Song Contest); they never saw my brother, Sonny, compete as a guard or shortstop on the respective Varsity teams.

Or I wear the school's colors as a Junior Varsity football, basketball and baseball and as a Varsity basketball and baseball competitor.

I suspect that when Billy, who was the most gifted athlete of all of us, was a student at Kamehameha, my parents also was unable to attend any of his activities.

They, however, religiously dropped off every other Friday afternoon our cleaned uniforms, laundry and a cake box of rice, omelet and Portuguese sausages.

Unfortunately for my Father, Kamehameha Schools replaced him as a father figure to his three sons. The absentee father syndrome would come to shape my attitude and feelings for a father who was to me, for all purposes, invisible.

But Kamehameha Schools could never replace our Mother.

While my Mother was a strong advocate for education, having completed just her 8th grade year at Mid Pacific High School as a funded scholar by the Judd family before her parents needed her back in Waikane, my Father, a Superintendent of the Hawaii Department of Education, and having completed just his 9th grade year at Erwin, Tennessee, was a milder advocate of post high school education for any of us.

He pulled himself up from the boot straps and believed his children should do the same; while he did not discourage my sisters from attending college, and they would have attained the highest honors had they attended, he was more tolerant regarding my brothers, Sonny and Billy, and my pursuit of a college education.

He applauded my brother, Sonny, who was completing his freshman year on a baseball scholarship and about to enter his second year at Winona State Teachers College, Winona, Minnesota.

On a Friday evening, my Mother accepted a long distance call from my brother in Winona, MN who was asking my Mother and Father for financial support so that he could enroll for his sophomore year; I happened to be in the kitchen during the phone call and privy to my parents' discussion.

My Mother, crying, had to inform Sonny that they could only send minimal funds as the businesses were not performing as well as they had hoped.

I wept quietly for my Mother knowing that her heart was broken; and for my brother knowing his dreams had just been shattered.

My brother returned home to Hawaii shortly thereafter, and though I was disappointed by his returning, I was more saddened that his fighting spirit may have been broken.

My parents grew apart in their later years as my brothers and sisters left the family home to start their own lives, raise their families, and build their own traditions and histories.

Communications between my parents had grown thin and were practically nonexistent; traveling together was an experience of the past; grandchildren had woven their own circle of friends and enjoyed examining life's many activities; and the holding of hands during strolls were a whisper of my parents' youth.

They each drifted noticeably and substantively from each other, and death was a welcomed consequence.

My Father, born 27 June 1912, died 3 April 1979 in Santa Clara, California while in residence with my sister Wanda and her family.

It is not until your parents have died that you begin to finally understand that you are now a parent, that you are now an adult and that you are responsible for your actions. You grow up rather quickly.

The eldest of the six of us was Betty Lou Kapuakela, born in 1 July 1936 and died so young at age 56 on 14 May 1992 due to breast cancer.

She was an extraordinarily beautiful woman who matured into a stunning lady, possessing all the exquisite gifts of physical grace, quick mind, dazzling smile and a keen understanding of human psychology.

She was also quick to leverage the shortcomings and weaknesses of those she needed to influence, perhaps at times not fully recognizing nor having a real understanding the impacts of her decisions.

But she lived her life simultaneously as a wife, mother, business leader, strategic policymaker, and social executive long, long before such terms as breaking the glass ceiling, empowerment of women, equal pay for women and equality of opportunities became the prevailing value system not only in our country but also worldwide.

She was at the leading edge of change, creating change rather than managing change. She was the Native Hawaiian of the future that *Kahu* Abraham Akaka had envisioned.

Betty Lou attended Kawananakoa Middle School from the 7th through 9th grades; she was then accepted as a sophomore, attended Kamehameha School for Girls, graduating with the Class of 1954.

Throughout Betty Lou's high school years, my Mother took her to hula lessons and recitals, and during one of her hula recitals in the Liliha district in 1950, she performed brilliantly and was instantly acclaimed as the next Ms. Hula Hawaii.

Sitting cross-legged on the floor with a perfect view of every hula dancer, I was in complete awe not only by her graceful interpretation of the hula but also her level of total confidence as an artist.

I knew then that she was special.

Encouraged by my Father, Betty Lou immediately enrolled in an accounting program and found employment at Hardwoods Hawaii as an account manager; over a 10-year span, she and Hardwoods Hawaii thrived; and she became the trusted ally of the full time *kama'aina* (native born) husband and wife owners of Hardwoods Hawaii who one day decided to retire and offered Betty Lou the right of first refusal.

Together with my parents, she bought out the owners and proceeded to expand the business, not only in the number of wood products that were marketed but also developed a corollary business, Garments Hawaii.

My Mother was the principal investor in both businesses, and my sister, Betty Lou, a 365/24/7 leader, manager, employee and strategic business developer who aligned the Waikiki hotels' growing tourist industry with guided tour buses who drove busloads of new tourists first to Garments Hawaii to purchase their Aloha attire and then to Hardwoods Hawaii to purchase gifts that could be shipped or delivered to their hotels to be hand carried with them back to the mainland.

She was a genius, but sadly during a time when women were not accorded their hard-earned value.

Married to Gilbert Ahlo, a 1954 classmate graduate of Kamehameha School for Boys, they were the parents of four wonderful children…Bonnie Lee, the first grandchild in the Cooper family now residing on Maui with her husband and young daughter; Brian Kau'i who passed away in 2016 leaving a two sons, Kala and Kaleo; Dwayne Kaimi who lives with his lovely wife on Oahu; and Darren Kaeloonalani who was tragically killed in an automobile accident as a teenager in 1984 (born 8 February 1966, died 29 March 1984).

All four grew up with a lot of independence simply because their parents were toiling every day to create successful businesses; but they were not without a lot of love that was supplied by my parents who became, each summer, the alter-parents who fed, bathed and provided 24/7 caring attention to each of them.

The strain on my parents was telling, especially on my Mother, as they worked all day at the businesses and now were the care givers of their four grandchildren.

However, my Father absolutely loved having the four grandchildren as they were an elixir potion that rejuvenated him; and the happy faces and laughter from each of them made the tough hours for my parents acceptable, if not gratifying.

Bonnie Lee and Kau'i, being the first grandchildren, struggled in their teenage years to find a balance to their lives as they were given much by my parents while asking for more attention and guidance from their own parents.

Bonnie has become a thoughtful wife and mother while Kau'i recently died as a result of his long battle with a kidney illness. Kaimi has always been the most solid of all, and the most sensitive like my Mother, though I suspect that Kaleo would have been the stable, fulcrum point for his three siblings.

Bonnie Lee and Kaimi retain their Mother's fighting spirit, her positive outlook on life, and her attitude that goodness can happen through hard work and compassion for others.

But Betty Lou could not sustain the constant cycle of growth.

In 1980 an accidental fire that started in a business several doors from Hardwoods Hawaii destroyed several businesses, including Hardwoods Hawaii; with limited fire insurance covering Hardwoods Hawaii, both my parents and Betty Lou relocated and re-started in one location both Hardwoods Hawaii and Garments Hawaii.

But the new location, adjacent to the Libby Pineapple Cannery, was several miles from the Waikiki hotels, thus making the ease of transporting newly arrived tourists from the hotels to the shops problematic.

The financing of the new start up, the making of new wood products, the collocation of both businesses and the energy required by the total team were constant concerns, but the single biggest adversary was the hotels' tourist industry – they were not accommodating of the new location because it did not support their sales marketing strategy.

Thus, in 1984 my sister was offered a buy out from an Asian buyer who had asked for a final decision; at lunch with the Asian buyer, it was clear that the buyer's intentions were, first, to downsize the workforce, and, second, find other efficiencies in the businesses; my sister and I walked to the car after lunch, and she asked my opinion.

I remember encouraging her to sell and walk away with something to show for her years of labor and return to our parents their properties that were being held as financial collateral.

Later that week, I was informed that both my Father and sister decided not to accept the offer even though they knew they were legally bound to pay a fee of approximately $100,000 to the proposed buyer should they walk away from the buyout offer.

My sister's rationale for not approving the buyout offer was that she could not see the valued employees of both businesses lose their jobs. Months later, both businesses were forced into bankruptcies, and all the employees lost their job.

About that time, 1984, the sky fell on my sister who developed breast cancer that she hid for some months because she could not afford the medical coverage and which eventually led to her death; the tragic automobile death of her youngest son, Kaleo; a divorce; a ruptured family; a new marriage to Tom Armstrong who took care of and stood by her during her battle with cancer; suffering to hold on to her sense of a meaningful life; and struggling to maintain her dignity.

But she did not quit; she kept fighting each day; she would not give in to the dark clouds that seemed never to leave her during those years.

She moved to Sisters, Oregon in 1990, to live out her last days; I drove to visit her from Portland, Oregon where I had been working with the Army Reserve unit.

When I saw her lying on the makeshift bed in the living room, so very, very thin, like a pencil, and lifeless; I leaned over and whispered in her ear:

> "It is OK to die; it is time; Mom and Dad
> are waiting for you; I shall see you once
> again."

I left Sisters, Oregon.

An hour later, her husband, Tom, called the family to announce that our sister, Betty Lou, had just passed.

The world that I had known was no more.

My older brother, Sonny, was my hero.

Born on 11 August 1938 and died on 13 October 2007, 19 months after his wife of forty-one years, Elizabeth, passed away (born on 21 July 1939, died on 19 January 2006); he is buried next to Elizabeth, and Elizabeth next to Elizabeth's mother, Mary Alencastre (born 25 December 1906, died on 8 December 1976).

Elizabeth was a natural, drop dead beauty who unfortunately suffered from a neurological disease called Machado-Joseph disease (MJD), also called spinocerebellar ataxia Type 3 (SCA3), passed on through the DNA of the affected female person to each generation in her family.

Through the prime of her life and into her later years, the disease eventually took her life.

Elizabeth was a bank teller at the Bank of Hawaii when Sonny stood at her window to make a deposit. I remember meeting Liz at a party in Kailua, and during a break in the energy of the party, I walked over to Sonny and said:

> "She is beautiful; you are lucky."

He just smiled.

Married several months later, they raised three handsome children, Kimberly who graduated from Kamehameha Schools; Robert Lewis Kawaiuli, II who graduated from Saint Louis High School; and Debbie who graduated from Kaimuki High School.

Each is doing extremely well and have made their parents very proud.

Kimi, for instance, is a certified life and health sales agent in several islands in Hawaii.

Debbie married Alika Kauaihilo, and they raised two wonderful daughters, Kahea and Ka'ulu who are now married with children of their own.

Kawai married Sonja, is currently the District Director of American Linen Supply in Honolulu, and they have raised two successful sons and a confident daughter.

They are dedicated to the memories of their parents, maintain a close affiliation with their cousins, and are always present at any Kamaka family function.

My brother and I shared so many memories growing old along together; he was always the protective big brother but who could be bitingly sarcastic whenever I got too much ahead of him in team sports.

For example, during the 1955-1956 basketball season, the Kamehameha Varsity Basketball team practiced during the Christmas holidays; he was the starting guard on Kamehameha Varsity Basketball team while I was the unofficial "towel and water boy" for the team.

At the end of every practice session, each team member shot twenty or more free throws; my brother made 15 free throw baskets; and I was challenged to shoot twenty free throws; I made sixteen.

Since we had to hitch hike back to Waikane after the practice session, and we did so twenty meters up from the then Piggly Wiggly Market and directly across the Nuuanu Baptist Church, he directed me to stand just off the sidewalk and do the hitch hiking while he rested on the black stonewall.

I did the hitch hiking for the entire Christmas holiday practice sessions.

Another time occurred when he, at age 13, started for the Palama Settlement baseball team of the Police Activities League; I, age 10, followed him to the practice field at Palama Settlement and watched transfixed at the smooth fielding movements of the infielders and the outfielders' effortless running, catching and throwing the fly balls back in to home plate.

I was standing along the edge of the right field when a ball was hit my way which I caught barehanded and made a throw all the way to home plate.

After that day, my brother made sure that I did not accompany him to his baseball practices.

My brother was a solid student at Kamehameha, entering his seventh grade year in 1950 and graduating in the top 10% of his class in 1956; he lettered in both Varsity Basketball and Baseball, was a model student, and well-liked by his classmates and appreciated by his teammates and coaches.

He worked diligently at everything – studies, sports, citizenship and adhering to the Schools' rules and policies.

During his senior year, he was selected by the Schools' active Army ROTC Instructors as the Corps Commander, the highest leadership position, of Kamehameha's ROTC Corps of Cadets, a distinguished honor equal to being the President of the Student Body or the Senior Class President or the Song Leader of the Senior Class, each chosen by one's peers or Senior Faculty members.

At that time I was an 8th grader living in I'olani Dormitory along with all 7th and 8th grade boarding students and had no appreciation nor understanding of my brother's accomplishment.

I just knew that every Saturday morning, about 9:00 am, we had to have our rooms fully ready for inspection by an Officer of the Corps staff.

One's Saturday Day-Pass to leave the grounds of the School depended on the demerits you received by the Inspecting Officer and the total demerits of the entire dormitory; thus, all dormitory students did their very best in preparing their rooms and their dormitories for the dreaded Saturday morning inspections.

On at least five Saturdays that year my brother was our dormitory inspecting officer; and as sure as the sun rises every day from the East, we had to re-stand a second inspection those five Saturdays; I was high on the list of room demerits each time, and it did not help any that I told my Mother that Sonny was picking on me, as my telling may just have increased the number of demerits my room received.

Perhaps it may not have the intended consequences by telling on your siblings.

On the athletic fields both he and I were much too busy establishing our playing positions on the teams to spend any time together; because we had different class schedules, we never bumped across each other during the day; since he was the top cadet and always surrounded by important Senior classmen, we never exchanged greetings during drills or our monthly Sunday parades which were fairly stirring events.

In fact, I don't ever recall chatting with him during his senior year, for as an 8th grader at Kamehameha School for Boys, you may observe but you never initiate a communication unless spoken to, especially to the vaunted seniors.

But the times we did share together bonded us like hoops of steel; however, it was not until I had founded the Pacific American Foundation that my brother and I threw aside obstacles to communication and became valued, trusted friends.

During January 1994 when I had returned home for what became for me a life changing meeting with Kahu Abraham Akaka, Sonny and I spent long evening hours huddled around his small round table in the dining room for 2-3 consecutive nights building, tearing down, rebuilding, repeated several times, until we were comfortable with the purpose, organization, the initial five-year plan and accounting systems of the newly registered Pacific American Foundation.

My brother's ideas were instrumental in shaping the strategic vision for the Pacific American Foundation, and his editing skills were influential in highlighting the specific actions that I had planned to use to introduce the Pacific American Foundation to Kenny Brown, Bob Oshiro, Irwin Cockett, Al Pauole, Monsignor Kekumano, Likeke Paglinawan, Mike Chun, Joe Souki, Jennifer Sabas, among others.

He retired early as the General Manager, American Linen Supply, because he did not want to uproot Liz, who was beginning to show early signs of the neurological disease, to take a promotion at American Linen headquarters located in Utah.

He also did not want to leave their three *mo'opunas* (grandchildren), Amanda, Kahea, Ka'ulu, nor Hawaii.

He left once for Winona State Teachers College in Minnesota and had no desire to leave once again.

His soul resided in Hawaii.

As he grew older, he loved playing golf and taking his boat, Kawai II, out in the ocean for fishing expeditions;

I was careful in helping him with the boat preparations, the exterior painting of his home, cleaning of his cars or working in the yard as he began to be a bit assertive and formed strongly held views on how to do things the right way.

He became less tolerant, more like our Father, as he found less and less things to do outside his home; and Liz required more and more of his time and attention.

But he was a fireball in advocating and raising funds for Multiple Sclerosis during Liz's early years battling the disease.

But the three of us enjoyed going to a Chinese or Japanese restaurant for cocktails and dinner; soon the waiters anticipated what we would order…comfort food…but always egg foo young at the Chinese restaurant and sashimi at the Japanese restaurant.

It was a time we shall always remember.

One of the relationships between my brother and me that I particularly regarded and appreciated was his complete dedication to being a big brother; there wasn't anything that I felt I owed an obligation to him; in fact, he carried a tremendous sense of personal obligation to our relationship; it was special.

Then he suffered a severe heart attack; with a 25% efficient heart, he confided in me that the cardiologist gave him a year or so; he, nevertheless, pushed himself to take care of Liz, helping her into the passenger seat as he drove me to the airport or to dinners, but he was fading as well.

Liz passed away first; then less than ten months after Liz had died, he joined her.

During the time after Liz had passed, he was wheel-chair bound but traveled with a classmate, immersed himself in the planning of his service, attending to every detail, to include the songs he wished played during his memorial.

But he also became a bit like Mark Twain who wrote his final book, The Damned Human Race, a satirical essay on mankind's moral insensitivity, written with an air of pessimism.

My brother made personal family decisions that strained relationships among his three adult children; made it difficult for Judy Mae and me to soothe hurt feelings; and minimized the strength of family cohesiveness that he and Liz had worked long and hard to develop.

He had been true to himself, his attitudes and beliefs; and it was difficult for me to watch the brother I loved take the approaches he chose in the last few months of his life.

I trust his three children will come to understand their Father.

At his gravesite, I placed a lei on his coffin as my heart communicated my feelings to him.

I stepped back, and suddenly my world had shrunk as I watched the casket being lowered into the earth - my best friend had truly died.

In the order of our births, I being the third (or fourth if you count the death of the brother who died at birth, Daniel Kaleoikaika), our sons, therefore, are next in line.

Troy Asao Kaleolani was born on 28 October 1962, a handsome baby with some ehu (reddish, sand color) in his hair and skin that was already tanned; always smiling, Troy was nearly the perfect baby, as first babies nearly are. Three things happened at his birth.

First, I was on crutches, having sprained my ankle playing basketball, when I drove our stick shift car, a convertible Hillman Minx, to Kapi'olani Maternity Hospital to pick up Kathy and our new son, Troy.

A child's car seat was not yet a requirement – it was not even a safety need or legal statue. And it was a very difficult, tough challenge to drive a stick shift car with a sprained foot, so best not to say any more.

Second, Amy, Kathy's older sister who was a RN working in Los Angeles, flew home to Honolulu to live with us to help with caring for Troy.

Kathy and I were living in a studio apartment in Varsity Circle, less than 2-3 blocks from the University, while Kathy continued to work for Akizaki (Peggy and Clarence) Employment Agency, along South King Street a block or two from the old Honolulu Stadium and positioned in front of the Shinto Shrine for which Clarence's brother was the Shinto Priest.

Though our living conditions were somewhat cramped, Amy decided to work the night shift at Kaiser Hospital in order to be home with Troy during the day while I finished my education and Kathy was at work.

It was a perfect arrangement.

Amy's decision was based in part on my father-in-law's, Kosuke, choice to follow his traditions that his daughters, Amy and Kathy, would only marry a man of the same race; he did not attend our Church wedding and forbade anyone from the Arakaki family to attend as well; as the senior family member, his decisions carried the weight of law for the entire family.

Consequently, Kathy was traditionally disowned by her father the day of our marriage, 16 June 1962, which meant that we were on our own.

Hence, Amy, who was strong willed, elected to return to Hawaii to help nurture Troy; and frankly, without Amy's loving care, we would not be where we are today.

But my mother-in-law, Haruko, found ways to communicate with us throughout the following months, oftentimes through Amy, finding a few moments of time to cuddle Troy and squeeze him tightly before leaving.

Little did I anticipate the next moment which, for Kathy and me, would be a life-changing experience.

And third, seven months after Troy's birth, May, which is traditionally celebrated as "Boys Day" by all Japanese people wherever they reside, Haruko called Kathy and asked her to bring Troy to their home in Tantalus by noon that day.

Elated, Kathy and Amy hurriedly got things packed for the drive while I, unfazed, did not even begin to understand the immense significance of the phone call and the ceremony that followed upon our arrival at their home.

Dutifully, we arrived about noon; Kathy, carrying Troy with Amy alongside, flew to the screen door while I gathered the baby bags and caught up with them; and just as I approached them, they entered, closing the screen door, leaving me to stand and observe the events from the outside.

Then the magic happened.

Kathy carried Troy the twenty steps it took to reach Kosuke and Haruko who were seated, cross legged, on either side of a two-tiered stand with Samurai dolls on both the lower platforms.

Upon receiving Troy, Kosuke and Haruko dressed Troy in an elegant Samurai outfit with a short sword, placed him on the top platform, and Kosuke spoke to the assembled family members welcoming Troy as the first Great Grandson and the first Grandson in the Arakaki family. And Troy flashed a huge smile to all!

As Kathy walked the twenty steps carrying Troy to her parents, on either side of the walkway were all of the Arakaki family members sitting on zabutans. Kosuke had reached out to all the family members for this enormously important event.

I was still standing outside the screen door looking in; as the fool I was, I did not understand the moment, nor the tradition so sacred to a Japanese family, nor the impact of my father-in-law's action to live by his traditions even though it hurt his immediate family, nor his accommodation to having fulfilled his obligation to tradition and that it was time to fulfill his obligation to his family, and nor the commitment of the entire Arakaki family to welcome the first Gaigin (non-Japanese), me, to the family.

It was a sacred time, a revered moment that must be shared with all families.

Troy, a graduate of Carlisle High School, Class of 1980; the United States Military Academy, Class of 1984; and Temple Law School, Class of 1993; is authorized to wear the Ranger, Airborne and Pathfinder tabs as well as the Combat Infantryman Badge (CIB) as a combat veteran of Desert Storm, having served as a Company Commander, 2/506th Infantry, 82nd Airborne Division, and is currently the Chief Executive Officer (CEO) of several companies.

Having been accepted into all three of the military ROTC scholarship programs and wait-listed at Princeton University, Troy traveled to Florida by train (we were residents of Florida at that time) during the Spring Break of his senior year at Carlisle to compete for one of the Congressional appointments to West Point.

He received instead a coveted Presidential Appointment to the United States Military Academy at West Point, choosing the

Military Academy two weeks after the Academy closed its certification process for the Plebe Class.

Fortunately, the Dean of Admissions, United States Military Academy, accepted Troy's late decision, and the rest is history.

Troy married the stunning Ellen, raised daughter Ellen who is now married with three children, and guided son, Nolan, who graduates in 2018 from Northwestern University with Honors, just wonderful young adults.

Nolan has been a role model for the other grandchildren, a position he seems to understand when his cousins look forward to being with him.

While I was away at Fort Benning, GA attending the requisite Infantry schools, Bradley Hideo Keikiokalani, born on 29 October 1963 at Kaiser Hospital, was a baby whose birth was fraught with challenges as his umbilical cord was wrapped around his neck; safely delivered, he was a happy, though very chubby, baby.

While Troy's birth brought adjustments, Brad's time with Kathy's parents was filled with laughter, giggles and lots of love.

Kathy, Amy and the two boys lived with Kathy's parents while I trained at Fort Benning, GA arriving home in Hawaii just before Christmas 1963.

I departed for Aschaffenburg, Germany, in January 1964, reporting for duty with the 1st Battalion, 7th Infantry "Cottonbalers" while Kathy and the two boys departed Honolulu in April 1964 to join me.

The tearful departure was made even more sad because we were not to see any of the Grandparents for three years during our time in Aschaffenburg, but Troy was able to attend Kinderschule (German Kindergarten) while Brad grew more chubby.

We have a picture of one of our Sunday walks in the park across from where we lived in the town of Aschaffenburg of Troy unable to get up because Brad was sitting on him. It was a very precious moment.

During our move to West Point in 1974, we drove through the mountains of Tennessee where Brad, upon seeing a herd of cattle on the hillside of a mountain, contemplated what he saw and commented to all of us in the car:

"Is that how we get lean beef?"

We burst out in laughter, but it was an early indication of Brad's incredible logical thinking and his eventual entrance into the engineering discipline.

Brad graduated from Fort Hunt High School, received a scholarship to Syracuse University for Mechanical Engineering in addition to an Air Force ROTC scholarship, and chose Auburn University in Alabama whose engineering program was closely affiliated with NASA's space efforts.

Brad loved Auburn, working as a part time volunteer in a Veterinarian clinic, went hunting when he could while finishing his Electrical Engineering degree in four and a half years, received his Commission as a Second Lieutenant in the Air Force with a first assignment to the Electronic Systems Command at Hanscom Air Force Base, Massachusetts, served his duty time and left the Air Force though he was selected for promotion to the rank of Captain, worked for an engineering firm at a work site on Kodiak Island, Alaska before entering Temple Law School where he graduated Magna Cum Laude in May 1992.

While a student at Auburn engineering, Brad spent the summer of his junior year at Sacramento AFB learning how to fly jet planes, but was not accepted for training as a pilot because of a sinus issue.

While at Hanscom AFB, he played soccer for the Base Soccer Team and hosted Ethan Scott and his Boston College roommates for beer and pizzas far more times than he had wished, though all enjoyed having an income-earner in Brad, with a car, in the immediate area.

Brad worked as an attorney in Philadelphia for a while; then started a law firm, Cooper, Morrison & Miller, LLC, with a partner in Philadelphia that today focuses on contract law and associated fields.

Brad is now the Chief Operating Officer (COO) for several companies.

Married to the striking Amanda, raising two sons, Liam Hideo Kekoaokalani, born 15 October 2009, who is just brilliant, and Rhys Koji Kapono, born 20 June 2012, who is simply dazzling intellectually and funny, and both are actively engaged in reading, archery, baseball, soccer, tennis, guitar and building amazing objects with their lego sets.

Ethan Scott Katsumi Kaleoikaika was born on 7 April 1966, five months before we departed Aschaffenburg, Germany and my first tour of duty in South Vietnam.

Ethan Scott would be unlike his two older brothers, much as Billy was unlike Sonny and me, but like Billy, devoted to his family and friends, and maturing over the years to recognizing his ethnic backgrounds with sensitivity and appreciation of those who went before.

Ethan Scott was his own person, dictating his style of clothes, choice of haircuts, sports participation, and possessed a special sense of verve.

He refused to attend Kamehameha Schools as an incoming Junior, saying he preferred to be with his Godparents in Aschaffenburg, Germany rather than reporting to Kamehameha in August 2002.

After six months at Leilehua High School in Wahiawa, he was accepted but refused to enter Punahou High School on an exception basis saying he was on the Varsity Basketball team at Leilehua High School and would not leave his teammates.

We applauded his sense of loyalty to his teammates.

Thus, he graduated from Leilehua High School, a distinction he relishes to this day; and a week before his graduation he received notification from Boston College that he was accepted as a student with the incoming Freshman Class.

Two events occurred at Leilehua High School that sealed his devotion to Leilehua.

The first occurred when he overheard a group of Polynesian students exclaiming how "nasty" Tor Kamata was as a professional wrestler and how much they seemed to admire him.

Ethan leaned over and remarked:

"He is my Uncle."

Prior to that revelation, any student from Schofield Barracks was a persona non grata; but in one remark, Ethan had suddenly become one of the local guys, one of them because his ancestry was of royal lineage since he was the nephew of Tor Kamata.

The second happened on the basketball court during practice and games.

Ethan's movements on the court, especially his jump shots and layups, were done flawlessly each and every time; his teammates began to call him "Silk," and that label has stood the test of time.

Leilehua's Varsity Basketball team played for the Hawaii State Championship against St. Louis High School in Ethan's senior year.

Four years later he was elected the Captain of Boston College's Volleyball Team.

Ethan had decided upon graduation to spend two years working with the farmers in South America as a way of serving others.

His other six roommates were headed to law schools, medical schools or graduate programs; and his Mother, though appreciative of Ethan Scott's desires, knew that if he did not go to a graduate program immediately and rather spent two years in service to others, he would not be able to fulfill his goals.

A 1976 TR6, a gift for entering law school (which he still has) and three years later, Ethan graduated from Catholic Law School in Washington, DC, the first of our family to receive a law degree; successfully passed the Bar Exam; served as a Captain for three years as a Judge Advocate, United States Army, in South Korea and Fort Meade, MD; worked as a Legal Counsel to three United States Congressional Representatives (Jim Saxon, R, NJ; Jim Weldon, R, PA; and Thomas Foglietta, R, PA); and completed his LLM degree in International and Comparative Law from Georgetown Law School in December 2002.

Ethan married the drop dead beautiful Jill Konz of Shelby, Iowa; together raising a son, Sebastian Carlo Katsumi Kaloikaika, born 20 July 2009, and a daughter, Gabrielle Rose Sachie Kawehikuokalani, born 20 December 2011, and currently is the owner and President of Haka, Incorporated.

Both grandchildren are highly intelligent, quick to learn, enjoy conversation with their peers and adults, love school (Ikaika says his favorite class periods are the Library and physical education periods, in that order); engage in ballet, piano and all sports, and loved by the wait staff and breakfast customers as Kathy and I religiously take them to Saturday morning breakfast at the Warehouse Restaurant in Old Town, Alexandria, Virginia.

Whenever Kathy and I look towards the future, we are comforted knowing that Ikaika, Kekoa, Evan, Kawehi, Kapono and Lauren have options that will challenge them to be more than they can be, as in the poem, <u>Andrea del Sarto</u>, by Robert Browning, the great 18th century English poet:

     "Ah, but a man's reach should exceed his grasp, or what's a Heaven for."

With appropriate courtesies, I depart from our Kamaka family to chat about my mother-in-law and father-in-law, Haruko and Kosuke, respectively.

Kosuke came to Hawaii as an eleven year old teenager and until 1974 was classified as a foreign citizen of Japan residing in the United States; while not an adverse status, he was not able to own property in the United States nor vote in any local, county, State or national election, among other unpleasant conditions.

In 1974 during my assignment to the United States Military Academy, I had asked to be assigned to the Military Attaché Service with duty in Japan; however, Infantry Branch informed me that I would be unable to serve in the Military Attaché Service because my father-in-law, Kosuke, was a foreign national.

Kosuke, upon being informed by Kathy of my dilemma, immediately signed up for citizenship status, underwent English training and citizenship education, and in 1975 became a U.S. citizen; his willingness to support my career has been a hallmark in my life.

And this story cannot go unrecorded.

In 1972 as Kathy, the boys and I were house hunting in North Kansas City, Missouri, because of my graduate program at the University of Missouri-Kansas City, Haruko sent us a check for the down payment for the home, money that she could not afford, yet like Kosuke who had since passed away, Haruko would sacrifice her well-being to support us.

We could not have purchased the home without Haruko's gift.

And this story cannot go unrecorded.

Kosuke and Haruko moved from their home to live with Kathy and the three boys while I served both combat tours in Vietnam.

Kosuke landscaped the entire yard, constructed a wall to hold the soil in place, built a stunning fishpond, took Troy every afternoon in his car to get a cone of ice cream, and was devoted to his grandchildren.

I recall an occasion during my first R&R to Hawaii in 1967 that was dramatic.

Kosuke had asked me to spend a few hours finding a rock for the fish pond that he had built in the patio of the home; so I put on my boots and rode with him just down the road where he parked, and we trudged up the side of the mountain until he found the precise stone – about 4 feet high and shaped like a needle with a wide base.

I lifted the stone which weighed about 90 pounds, gingerly stepped my way down the mountain, and barely lifted it into the trunk of the car knowing that it would take a miracle to get it out of the trunk.

Arriving at the home, I took a deep, deep breath and lifted the rock from the trunk of the car, walked down the six step to the fish pond, all the while hearing Kosuke telling me to be careful not to drop the stone.

I managed to place the stone at the head of the fishpond, entirely exhausted as I sat down in a chair in the patio.

Kosuke, on the other hand, sat on his heels smoking a cigarette for nearly 12-15 minutes; the hushed silence did not diminish my perspiration.

But then Kosuke stood up, walked over to the stone, and moved no more than an inch to the right.

The transformation of the entire fishpond was dramatic.

It was the most poetic sight I had seen in nearly seven months; it was simply beautiful and strikingly spectacular.

I stood up, and for the first time realized I was in the presence of a special person.

However, let me go back to September 1966 and the evening of my departure from Honolulu International Airport to South Vietnam for my first of two combat tours.

I was busy the early evening packing my gear into the duffle bag at my in-laws home and did not recognize that three other Japanese Americans had gathered in the living room and with Kosuke, who was a *Sensie* (teacher) of the Japanese shamisen, had begun to play Japanese songs on their shamisen; they continued to play for nearly ninety-minutes.

Finally packed, I said my goodbyes, and with Kathy drove to the airport.

Only years later did Kathy mention that my father-in-law had asked his students to honor me by playing Japanese songs that evening, an honor reserved for the Japanese Samurai of earlier centuries as they were preparing for combat.

I cried.

Kosuke and Haruko were rare gifts; they were irreplaceably unique; they were one of its kind; and I shall always love them.

And these special occasions cannot go unrecorded.

Kosuke and Haruko were exceptional parents who raised Andy whose son, Charles, is now a physician in Honolulu; Charles who is a graduate of Marquette, received his Dental degree from Loyola of Chicago, and did graduate study at the University of Southern California; Amy who is a Registered Nurse; and Katherine who raised our three sons, with enormous love, impressive insights regarding nature, modeled life's steadfast values with civility.

As Kathy and I look back over the past seventy-five years, we are very grateful for many, many wonderful events in our lives, but probably the most satisfying are that our three sons have developed into kind and superb persons, graduated with distinction from their universities and served their country with compelling and dedicated honor.

Judy Mae Puahaunani, born 15 March 1943, died 2 December 2009, was an amazing lady; she was without question the intellectual giant of all six of us, and in my view, of all 27 Kamaka first cousins.

She was without peer in logic, in critical analyses, in numbers, in comprehension, in communication and in strategic conceptualization.

But what separated her from all of us was her innate ability to understand people, to reach out to others but not be drawn in, to stand apart while being a part of the situation.

Unlike my sister Betty Lou, Judy Mae was not a butterfly exuding graceful beauty but a more arresting, striking looking woman who was also an extraordinary person, more a kind steel fist wrapped in a soft velvet glove.

When she spoke, we did not interrupt. When she suggested, we followed; when she was angry, we escaped into a hull defilade position.

She did not tolerate fools.

But she was a soft touch, a pushover; focus your argument around the edges of a deliberation, agree to her basic position, and she would accept the changes you recommend.

However, fail to carry out the agreement and best to leave the State of Hawaii rather than face my sister's irritation and displeasure.

She was the quintessential Native Hawaiian of our generation, living as close to the values of those who went before; exuding a generosity and warmth that spilled over everyone she met; giving freely of her talents and skills to preserve the Kamaka family;

establishing a well-earned and deserved reputation as a luau expert and gourmand; raising her nieces and nephews with such love and discipline that they are today representatives of the values, accountability and courtesies she taught; and completely unselfish with her assets, resources and possessions.

A 1961 graduate of Kamehameha School for Girls, she was the only one of the six of us to attend Waiahole Elementary School through the 6th grade before being accepted and becoming a 7th grade boarding student at Kamehameha School for Girls.

Judy married Ralph Mutsuo Tsutsui of Waikane in 1971 in the Waikane Congregational Church; honeymooned in Venice, Italy; returned home to Waikane where they have lived ever since; and raised a stunning daughter, Ursula Brigitte.

Ursula, born on 22 July 1975, graduate of Mid Pacific Institute, an academic-oriented independent high school in Hawaii; earned a BS degree, University of Portland; and received her MA with Highest Honors, University of Hawaii – Manoa, who in 2003 married Jason Quan (20 February 1971) of Oregon and together are the proud parents of Evan, 7 years, (10 September 2009) and Lauren, 5 years (17 April 2012).

The children will lead the next generation of Kamakas, for they are brilliant, courteous, warm, gracious and possess an incredible love of learning.

Muts, born 9 August 1941, was an unexpected diamond in the rough; we grew up together less than a mile apart, but our high school and later years separated us by significant geographical distances.

Having returned from a job in the Pacific, he was introduced to Judy by Gilbert Ahlo, my brother-in-law; and after a period of courtship, they were married.

Recently, Muts and I were enjoying our Saturday morning breakfast at Zippy's in Kaneohe, when I asked him what one thing he did in his life that was a life changing event.

Muts, who should never be mistaken for a communicator, grabbed his cup of coffee and at the same time said:

"I married your sister Judy."

It has been eight years since Judy died; and neither of us have reconciled our souls to her passing; I certainly have not forgiven her for dying so young; and Muts misses her interminable comments about everything in life.

So we two senior citizens, with a Zippy's 10% value card, spend our Saturday mornings talking about the same things over and over and over.

It is sad, not so much that Judy is not there, but we, the living, know we have a short runway, that we must endure.

The loneliness we share is just barely perceptible, but after nearly 8 years of just the two of us sitting at the same table at the same Zippy's at the same hour, other patrons recognize that life's once bright candle is dimming for us.

Muts and my first cousin, Miguel, graduated together from Castle High School in 1959; and when we three get together for coffee, they animatedly recall their high school days, hitch hiking from Waikane every day to Castle High School in Kaneohe, oftentimes arriving well into the second period of the day with the rationale they so often responded to their teachers:

"Try hitch hiking every day, and see if you can do any better."

They graduated because they earned enough education credits, not because they were socially graduated. I mention this story simply because education was and is today so very important to both of them, even though they arrived late to school every day.

Kathy, the three boys and I joined several hundred well-wishers at the marriage ceremony at Waikane Congregational Church on a late Saturday afternoon; unknown to us, Judy had wanted Uncle Willie to escort her down the aisle but he, along with Aunty Ka'akau, insisted that the privilege belonged to my Father.

I was somewhat shocked to see my Father and Judy arm in hand walking down the aisle.

I was not prepared for my Father's appearance; bald for most of his adult life, he was wearing a wig; the wig looked goofy, and my Father looked goofy! It was the topic of small talk for months and months.

Yet credit to my Father who carried himself proudly throughout the ceremony and never faltered.

Whenever I was fortunate enough to visit with Judy and Muts in Waikane, we would sit outside and spend hours speaking about the "children" – Troy, Brad, Ethan, Urs, Michael and Kanoa – never acknowledging that they were in their thirties and forties with their own children; but reflecting on the memories of the sacrifices we made, never openly, never directly, only indirectly, to get them to where they are today.

Judy and Muts were especially humbled by their good fortune to align themselves with T. Iida Construction Company whose two principal leaders, Henry Iida and Alvin Iida, believed in loyalty, hard work and sacrificing for their children's pursuit of education.

Muts was the wage earner who was the principal construction site foreman, knowledgeable of all facets of construction, including reading architectural blue prints and fine carpentry, while Judy managed the earnings with such skill that she often notoriously, and at times purposefully, mixed GAAP (Generally Accepted Accounting Principles) with gap (finding holes) which led to amazing accounting logic and psychologically defensive mechanisms; she found techniques of investing and methods of accounting that I affectionately termed risk taking, though others may have found them to be on the margin of and in the gray area of accounting.

But she and Muts fully paid for Ursula's high tuition costs at the prestigious Mid Pacific High School and the even more prestigious, and costly, University of Portland, Oregon.

And they did so without taking any loans or leveraging their home or asking for assistance. They sacrificed their quality of life for the one thing that once achieved, no one can take it away – education.

During Ursula's sophomore year at the University of Portland, I was invited to speak at a health symposium in Portland; arranging a visit with Ursula, we spent a day together with her two college classmates, Liza Chun and Stacia Murray.

Two events happened that day which significantly impacted my opinion of Ursula.

First, the Honda provided to Ursula by her parents had a fuel shut off mechanism installed, at the insistence of my sister, in the trunk in the event that if someone tried to steal the Honda, somehow the fuel mechanism would be activated.

Driving in the middle of downtown Portland, the Honda fuel mechanism activated; the car stopped suddenly; and we four had to push the car to the side of the very busy intersection.

Unfazed, Ursula issued instructions to Liza and Stacia with such confidence that I realized she was the spitting image of her mother, my sister. Thus, she had things under control; I was just an appendage.

The second incident occurred the next day when Ursula and I visited her Nursing Laboratory where I met her Professor.

In an exchange of data that only an Uncle as I would be asking, I drove away from the campus to the airport completely in awe of Ursula's educational accomplishments; the intensity of esteem that colleagues and Professors had for her; and how proud her parents would be of the results of their sacrifices in the name of education, respect for others, and personal accountability.

Commitment was never in lower capitals for Judy; when Aunty Ka'akau took ill and steadily become immobile, it was Judy who tended to Aunty's every healthcare requirements and personal needs; and Judy never, ever complained; rather, she seemed to grow stronger and more tolerant of the vagaries that life delivers when you least expect it.

She took care of our Grandniece, Jessica, and her *hanai* Grandson, Kahner, during their teenage years; she reached out to our brothers Sonny and Billy weekly asking about their health (both brothers had suffered crippling heart attacks); she arranged hospice care for Sonny during his last weeks, recruiting family members who were willing to kokua, and she accompanied Muts on travels to the mainland.

And all along her care for others, she never brought up the severe heart surgery she underwent at age forty; nor was she a complainer when she suffered a setback during one of their travels and had to be rushed to a local hospital.

Perhaps it was her calling to be a steel fist wrapped in a pure velvet glove.

She was a human being that we, the living, reverently refer to a person who walks by you as "once in a lifetime."

Billy, born on July 1945 and died on 5 December 2011. The youngest of the three of us boys, he was the best of us all in any measurable way...a gifted athlete; the most generous of his time and wealth; the easiest with whom to have a conversation on any topic; a very gentle, considerate Native Hawaiian whose welcome to his home was reminiscent of my Aunts' greetings in Hawaiian, "Hele mai ai."

Billy entered Kamehameha School for Boys as a 7th grader in 1957, graduating in 1963; he was his own person during his high school years, preferring to set his own agenda in the classroom, on the athletic fields, on adhering to the competitive nature of ROTC and to the governing rules of Kamehameha.

On one occasion, our Father, who was at work, was called by the medical clinic at Waikiki directing him to pick up Billy from the clinic as they had completed stitching his gash received from surfing. Somewhat befuddled, my Father drove over to Waikiki, picked up Billy, drove to Kamehameha, and dropped off Billy.

Later, my parents were called by the administration at Kamehameha to inform them that Billy had received a bunch of demerits that required him to walk them off around the Paki Hall basketball court for the next several Saturday mornings.

Asking what had happened, my parents were told that Billy had slipped away from the campus during school hours to go surfing, that he had received a gash requiring stitches and had returned to the campus.

Little did my Father realize he was aiding a truant!

I was honored to be his Best Man at his first wedding to Sandy, a private ceremony that took place in Waikane during a time when Waikane seemed to be the whole world for the two of us.

A year later their precious daughter, Darlene, was born who followed her father everywhere, often spent her growing years at Judy Mae's home, and was the happiest, most beautiful, young girl.

Several years later Billy and Sandy divorced, and the struggles of divorced parents seemed to swallow Billy's time.

But then he found the exquisite Penny Mikie, his current wife, and he began to smile once again as they became the proud parents of two highly successful sons, Michael Elliot Keoni, who graduated from Punahou High School, Class of 1994, and from the University of San Diego in 1999; earned the Honolulu Advertiser's First Team Soccer Honors as a Junior; and a member of the first ever Honolulu Advertiser's Hawaii State All-Soccer First Team during his senior year.

Jason Patrick Kanoa, a graduate of Kamehameha Schools, Class of 1998, as well as Gonzaga University in 2002, was a member of the Hawaii State All-Soccer First Team his senior year; starting defensive Safety on the Varsity football team; and selected as the Male Athlete of the Year during his senior year at Kamehameha.

They inherited Billy's athletic DNA and Penny's academic spirit and her fiercely competitive edge.

Michael today is emerging as an inspirational business leader in Hawaii; Kanoa has advanced his interest in soccer into a pronounced, abundant success as a business in Spokane, Washington.

I recall having an early breakfast with Michael, who was in his second year at University of San Diego, during a coordinating trip to San Diego; though it was early, both of us arrived nearly on time; and I could tell by Michael's demeanor that he was not especially happy getting a free breakfast so early in the morning.

Nevertheless, we worked our way through breakfast with moments of clarity from Michael in response to my endless inquisitive questions.

I am sure Michael was ecstatic when we hugged and said our goodbyes.

Should Michael and Kanoa, together with their cousins –Troy, Brad, Ursula, Kawai, Bonnie, Kimi and Ethan – harness their unified capabilities, endless successes will come their way.

During our later years, we three brothers often played golf together with the fourth partner either one of their sons, Kawai or Michael; Sonny and Billy were serious golfers, approaching each golf swing with appropriate practice swings, a winning mental attitude and very few shakes of the hips just prior to hitting the golf ball.

I, on the other hand, came to enjoy the scenery, move the ball to a better lie, and took more mulligans than allowed; it infuriated my brothers whose game at or about the 11th hole eventually looked like they were beginning players. Only my nephews enjoyed the game, swinging freely and not at all bothered by the game within the game.

The time after the golf outing will always be remembered as the "Brothers' Time."

On one golf outing, Billy noticed I was using equipment and a golfing bag from the Club; he went into the Club and came out with a white, Ping pro-type golf bag which he bought for me; such was the generosity of my brother; a few years ago I gave the bag to my eldest son, Troy, who had taken up golf. It remains in the family today.

We had invested in two Waikane properties, subdivided them and placed on the properties two duplex apartments which required extensive renovations. We all participated with Muts providing the tools, equipment and the renovation supplies while we provided the skilled labor, or in my case, just labor.

Billy and Penny were always the principal workers, skilled in emplacing cabinets, studs, walls, window frames, doors, sanding and painting; regardless of the work schedule arranged by Judy, they were prompt, brought lunch for all and never complained regarding the physical labor.

Penny was especially cheerful while Billy was focused on accomplishing the work objectives for the day. At times it was humorous seeing both of them covered in dust with a white mask over their nose and mouth.

Sonny, Gilbert and Billy even thought of going into home renovation business, selecting "Waikane Home Renovation Experts" as a name for their nascent company. Fortunately for all of us, the company never got beyond their talking stage.

Billy transformed his athletic gifts into coaching soccer as Michael and Kanoa got older; Kathy and I would often watch his coaching of games or practice sessions at Kapi'olani Park and at Kaneohe.

He communicated with all his players in a way that only real, successful coaches do, but the amazing factor was that though he spoke little to the parents, what he said was received as gospel by the parents.

Like their sons and daughters, they believed and respected Billy, or Coach.

He was truly an incredible Native Hawaiian.

Billy, who one morning was experiencing heart pain, had asked Kanoa to drive him to Castle Memorial Hospital who then rushed him to Kuakini Hospital where he underwent an immediate quadruple heart bypass surgery.

I happened to fly in to Honolulu that day from Guam, and joined Penny, my sisters, Betty and Judy, along with their husbands, and Sonny and Liz at the hospital as Billy, after a 4-hour surgery, was wheeled into his recovery room.

I had witnessed both brothers immediately after their surgery, and my sister, Betty Lou, in cancer recovery, and to this day I can still see each one with a number of tubes and breathing apparatus hooked to them.

It's a sight my parents would not have wanted to see.

Billy, after more than six months, recovered sufficiently to be hired by TSA for passenger security at Honolulu International Airport. Between physical therapy and his work at TSA, he seemed resigned to a slower pace, less golf and less coaching. Penny kept him actively involved with the boys, the family, their friends but she sensed that his runway had shortened.

One Saturday in November as I drove to our parents' and siblings' gravesites in Kaneohe to place flowers, I resolved to stop by to see Billy and Penny whom I had not visited in 2-3 years.

Billy was just admitted to Queens Hospital for observation, so I stopped by to see him, arriving at his room within 20-minutes of his discharge. Chatting as we walked to his car which Penny had driven to the valet parking in front of the hospital, we hugged each other and said our good byes.

They drove off.

Two weeks later Billy died, on his own bed, in his own home, with Penny and Michael standing by him and a Priest administering the last rites.

Wanda Leen, the youngest of us all, born on June 30, 1948 and died on May 2, 2000, graduated from Kamehameha School for Girls with the Class of 1966.

Married to David Carroll, raised two daughters, Alissa (the eldest) and Andrea (the youngest), and a son, David, all three currently reside in Oklahoma City, OK.

Wanda enjoyed the benefits of our parents having already experienced the terrible teen years from the five of us, but not all benefits are really plusses; though resilient and family-oriented, she did not face the struggles, and learned from them, as the rest of us had with our Father.

Hence, she may have missed out on the toughness and the competitive spirit that seemed to wrap themselves around Betty Lou or Judy Mae; but she was thoroughly strong when it came to her family.

After Mom died, Dad spent his last years in residence with Wanda as she was caring and sensitive.

I missed Wanda's graduation from Kamehameha as I was returning from Germany enroute to my first of two tours in Vietnam; however, during my first R&R (rest and recreation) from Vietnam in Hawaii, Wanda asked to have lunch with Kathy and me; she and David announced their plans to get married and asked for our support which we immediately said "yes."

She was really putting in place a strong support team of her brothers and sisters before she and David went to see my parents and asked for their blessing.

Wanda and David worked for Hardwoods Hawaii for two-three years, then decided to move to Sacramento, California. It was a sad time for my parents who doted on their children.

While in Sacramento City, David worked for and eventually he and Wanda bought the Singer sewing machine repair business in Sacramento City with financial support by Judy Mae and Muts.

They worked long hours to make a success of the business, but the economy in Northern California, coupled with the reduction of seamstresses and others who depended on a sewing machine, unfortunately led to the failure of their business.

When we sold our parent's property in Waikane, all financial obligations were settled between Wanda and David and Judy and Muts.

Rather than returning home to Hawaii, Wanda and her family decided to remain in Sacramento where Brad, during his junior year at Auburn University, reported to McClellan Air Force Base for flight training and spent a day with Wanda and her family.

Recently Alissa has been in communications with Kathy and me; she seems to have a spirit to do well, accepts challenges, an excellent writer, sensitive but standing on her own two feet. She will do well.

Her siblings, David, now married, and Andrea are doing equally well at their jobs, thriving and comfortable residents at their new home State of Oklahoma.

12. Rachel Nainoa Kamaka, 1917 – 1992

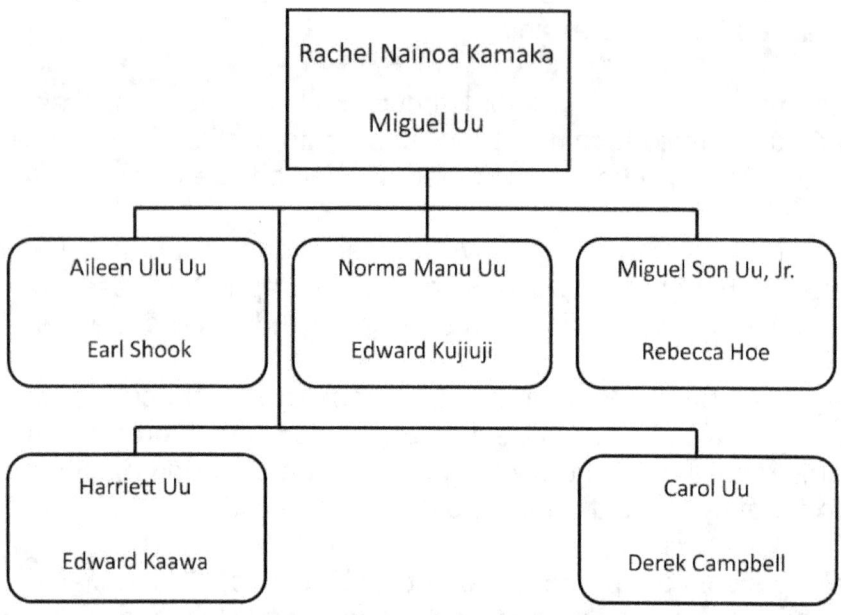

Aunty Rachel, the youngest of the eleven (11) Kamaka siblings, was the most Hawaiian of all - her demeanor, sensitivity to others, quiet speaking habit, graciousness, and pure spirit of Aloha.

I saw Aunty Rachel as my alter-Mother, an Aunt to whom I went when I needed to spend time away from home; Aunty Rachel always offered me something to eat, especially poi; and I always enjoyed my cousins, her children, and always their son, Miguel, or Son, who was my age.

Aunty married Miguel (Mickey) Keliikupakako Uu, whose brother, Uncle Charlie, had a different last name, Charles Ho'omana, who married Aunty Helen, a local Japanese, and together Aunty Helen and Uncle Charlie were absolute devotees of professional wrestling. Uncle Charlie was an expert car repairman and often would help me with the obstinate 1950 Studebaker, my first car, and now a classic car among those who are collectors.

Uncle Mickey worked as a school engineer in Kaneohe, Monday through Friday, and on the weekends was busy working on various projects around the house; he never required Son, or me since I was at their home a lot, to assist him; but he was the hardest working Native Hawaiian I have ever met in my life.

Aunty was always a very busy stay-at-home Mom, tending to not only her children but also all the Kamaka cousins; if we were not at Aunty Thelma's home, one could certainly find us camped out at Aunty Rachel's home.

Coming and going, going and coming, we wore out the hinges on the front and back doors, such was the graciousness of Aunty Rachel.

Aunty and Uncle raised four girls in order of Aileen Ulu; Norma Manu; Harriett; Carol and one son, Miguel Jr., or Son.

Ulu was the same age as my sister Betty Lou, graduated from Castle High School, enjoyed life, had a quick wit, married and lived on the mainland for a few years before returning home with four children, and died suddenly from a heart complication.

Manu, a year or two older than I, graduated from Castle High School, assertive and hardworking, married Edward Kujiuji, lives in Honolulu with her husband and grown daughter.

Harriett, graduated from Castle High School, always the beautiful and proper lady, married Ed Kaawa, lived in Waikane, raised two lovely daughters; Harriett had a special kinship with my sister Judy Mae, especially through her battle with cancer, until the cancer took her.

Son graduated from Castle High School, is a combat veteran with a 105 howitzer unit, the 1st Battalion, 21st Artillery, 1st Cavalry Division, one of the first combat units to land in South Vietnam in 1965; married Becky Hoe from Hakipu'u, raised two daughters and a son as well as two Granddaughters who graduated from Kamehameha Schools, lost his wonderful wife to cancer, and is now fully retired living on the Kona Coast, Big Island.

And then there is Carol, who graduated from Castle High School, warm and outgoing, played the drums, married Derek Campbell, raised five superb, gifted children, one of whom is named Ulu, after her Aunt, and graduated from the University of Hawaii – Manoa, as a President's Scholar. And every one of their children is a magnificent singer and musician.

Uncle Mickey purchased a classic 1950 2-door, light blue Ford Thunderbird which was the envy of all the Kamaka cousins. Imagine a Native Hawaiian who perhaps never left Oahu, never got on an airplane, and one day driving home an automobile that was beyond our reach…way, way beyond our reach. He became an instant hero among the Kamaka family.

I was at Fort Meade, MD when Aunty Rachel passed away on 29 May 1992; I wished I had been there for her and my special cousins; but such is life, for as I have learned over the years, life happens when you least expect it.

13. The Modern Kamaka Ohana – The Challenge

Throughout this historical narrative, there were indications, previews of the challenges that my generation of Kamakas faced, challenges that are today no more different for the 21st century generation of Kamakas.

Except in one degree…the challenges are more sophisticated requiring a higher dedication of educational and technological skills, skills that seem to evade most of the Kamakas of all generations, and perhaps one could even extend the shortcomings to many Native Hawaiians today.

Yet the generation of Kamakas of my Mother's time was the last generation of real Native Hawaiians who lived their culture, practiced their traditions, spoke their language with all its hidden meanings, and understood the spirituality of nature.

On a beautiful Sunday morning in 1995, while enjoying a tennis game at a private home in Aina Haina, the host asked me two questions.

First, why did I start the Pacific American Foundation, and second, how many Native Hawaiians did I expect to help?

The host, Bob, was slightly older than I, and unknown to me until later that day that he and my Sister Judy were co-workers years ago; but the revealing fact was that he was smitten by her; and hence, the invitation to play tennis on his home court with his friends on a beautiful Hawaii Sunday morning.

My responses summarized the answer given by W.E.B. Dubois in an article he wrote that was published in the *Negro Problem* in 1903 when asked why he thought African Americans needed higher educational support in order to become leaders of their race and contribute significantly to the United States.

He responded by describing a program he called the Talented Tenth; that is, if just one of ten African Americans had the opportunity to succeed educationally, they will form the vanguard of millions of African Americans who will become *good and industrious* citizens of our great country (italicized phrase quoted from Princess Bernice Pauahi's handwritten thirteenth codicil of her will).

Rather than a focus principally on industrial education, DuBois argued that there must be a system in place for all Americans, especially African Americans, that must include technical, industrial, classical and schools of higher education that promote intelligence, broad sympathy and knowledge of the world so that one can comprehend, appreciate and accommodate, as appropriate, changes that always occur regardless of where one is or one's position in life.

Our Native Hawaiian Gods should have paid attention as Kahu Akaka's Tutuwahine so accurately revealed as DuBois wrote these thoughts while a resident of New York City in the 1900's.

I viewed then, and still do today, that the Pacific American Foundation could advance the belief, of what had been envisioned by other Native Hawaiian leaders who had gone before me, that through rigorous learning from early childhood through the levels of higher education, and an organization that was passionate about such a purpose, of just a tenth of Native Hawaiians we could achieve unlimited success in cultural, academic, governance, business, public policy, finance, social, healthcare and legal fields, among others.

Bob nodded in agreement, and then shared with me his personal admiration for my sister Judy.

I wasn't quite sure whether my logic or my attractive sister won the day!

On or about 1985 an editorial appeared in the Honolulu Advertiser which highlighted the few Native Hawaiians who had done well in their professions; it was shown to me by a Native Hawaiian colleague, and as I read the editorial written by respected journalist, a seed was planted for such a book as The Legacy Lives On.

In 2010 Andrew K. Poepoe, Muriel Morgan Gehrman, and Ednette Tam Chandler compiled a book entitled, The Legacy Lives On, that a few of us had been strong advocates for several years for a listing of significant contributions by Native Hawaiians.

The book contains a summary of the contributions in education, military, business, religion, government, culture and arts by Native Hawaiians in the State of Hawaii; though not inclusive of the many other Native Hawaiians who have made noteworthy contributions, the book nevertheless points to the basic principle that education can be a game changer, for it is education upon which lives are built and dreams fulfilled.

Each of the one hundred Native Hawaiians in the book are but representative examples of many other successful Native Hawaiians who have excelled in their professions, some in more than one profession, "and who are role models for future generations of Native Hawaiians."

By celebrating the successes and contributions of Native Hawaiians, especially those who can relate their accomplishments back to their educational journey, then we celebrate not only their accomplishments but also their dedication to education, to learning, from which all journeys begin.

Alexander Pope, the great 18th century English poet, wrote that,

"Tis education form the common mind; just as the twig is bent, the tree's inclined."

Education provides the opportunity to learn and develop leadership skills, but education alone is not the panacea to filling a void in leadership positions.

While education does provide the scenario for leadership examples, case studies, illustrations and discussions, it does not provide the mentoring and field experiences critical to developing the proper attitude and understanding the impact of positive leadership skills.

Equally important, however, is the sensing of the situation as to when to exert leadership, how to inject the right amount as well as the style of leadership to influence the situation appropriately, and how to measure the impact of leadership skills used for that situation.

Leadership skills, both positive and negative, are learned essentially through education but nurtured by actual experiences in real leadership positions, whether such positions are appointed and confirmed, as in government positions, or selected, as generally in most other situations.

Role modeling, however, offers a unique experience to learn leadership by example, for it combines the teaching matrix of "See-Do-Repeat."

Native Hawaiians possess a rich cultural tradition of learning that emphasizes role modeling, or tactile learning, which encourages observation, action and repetition. Such is how I learned how to patch a fishing net and build a fishing trap, among other things.

But there was also the learning that occurs between the covers of books, the formal education acquired in classrooms taught by devoted teachers and encouraged by steadfast parents and relatives.

My generation of Kamakas took the leap, encouraged by our parents, from the "See-Do-Repeat" matrix towards the more rigorous classroom education that develops critical thinking skills, how to think not what to think; but of the twenty-seven Kamaka cousins of my time, less than 10% leveraged higher education, regardless of the reasons.

Without the learning that occurs within a classroom, however valuable or not, there is little hope of an offer of credible leadership positions simply because we are not prepared nor understood the basic elements of leadership skills, and thus are not likely candidates for any leadership position.

The ability to think through problems and sort out the details in somewhat logical patterns leads to a healthy life style, and when Native Hawaiians practice a healthy life style, healthy Native Hawaiian communities develop and thrive.

Preventing the abuse of alcohol and drugs, paying attention to proper foods and quantities become good habits, and good habits lead to longer and more productive lives.

As we think about the value of continuous learning after four-five years of formal education at a university or community college or junior college, the impacts occur in various ways, as choosing a healthy life style; balancing the many incursions on your time; managing stresses that accompany daily life; reaching important family decisions that require relevant data and intimate collaboration; making significant financial decisions as buying a home or renting or moving or taking on a new job in a new industry; planning thoughtfully for retirement years; leveraging your internal experiences on being a dedicated friend or parent; deciding on how and where your children will be educated, among many other choices made somewhat more acceptable simply because of higher education allows you to think critically and act more decisively.

The men of my generation of Native Hawaiians, as evidenced by my own siblings, tend to die before age seventy, just as they are ready to be *Kupunas* (elders) and mentors to others; while our Native Hawaiian women live a bit longer, they too are challenged to share their *mana'o* (wisdom) as illnesses during their adult years take their toll.

Kenneth Brown always reminded me during our talk story sessions that building healthy Native Hawaiian communities takes a lot of effort, requires all of us to *kokua* (help), and the results would be potentially impressive contributions because Native Hawaiian men and women can live to an age where they can give back to others. Kenny was always there to echo the fact that of the three indigenous races (American Indians, Native Alaskans, and Native Hawaiians) of our country, we, Native Hawaiians, are the closest in time to nature. It seems to me that we Native Hawaiians, because we are closer to nature, and therefore look closer into nature, knowledge will be more readily visible.

The challenge for the next generation of Kamakas, my nephews, nieces, second and third cousins, is that the world they now live in changes all too quickly.

However, changes can be identified and accommodated; understanding the current and future impact of change takes learning that principally comes from education, education that starts with early childhood and continues until death calls.

"You must be the change you wish to see in the world." (Ghandi)

They are faced with another challenge, and that is developing the leadership skills that allow them to understand the purpose of parenting, mentoring, coaching, teaching, role modeling and cheer leading play in building solid, good and industrious, meaningful lives that permit them to one day reach back and help others.

Many who teach leadership contend that it is both an art and a skill; while we have codified many of the skills into situational exercises and "what now" situations, there is a distinct element that comes from the *na'au* (seat of intelligence, thought, instinct) that allows one to recognize that when one door shuts, another window opens; that like art, one knows art when one sees it, similar to leadership instinct, for when one feels right, then it can be so.

Native Hawaiians, it seems to me, have this instinct, some more than others, and it is this group that when combined with skills learned through education and our respect for nature, can become event making leaders rather than eventful people.

If there is any one value to be gained from this narrative, it will depend on how the readers apprehend the value of these pages.

Perhaps there is more than one message with which the readers may take from this reading, but surely much will depend on where the readers want to go, how they plan to get there, and who can help them get to where they want to be.

The journey is equally critical as the results.

EXTENDED CHAPTER – THE COOPER FAMILY

This extended chapter represents a more detailed ancestry of my siblings' children who now have children of their own. It is as accurate as the input from my nephews and nieces, sufficient for understanding the genealogy of the generations that follow my parents.

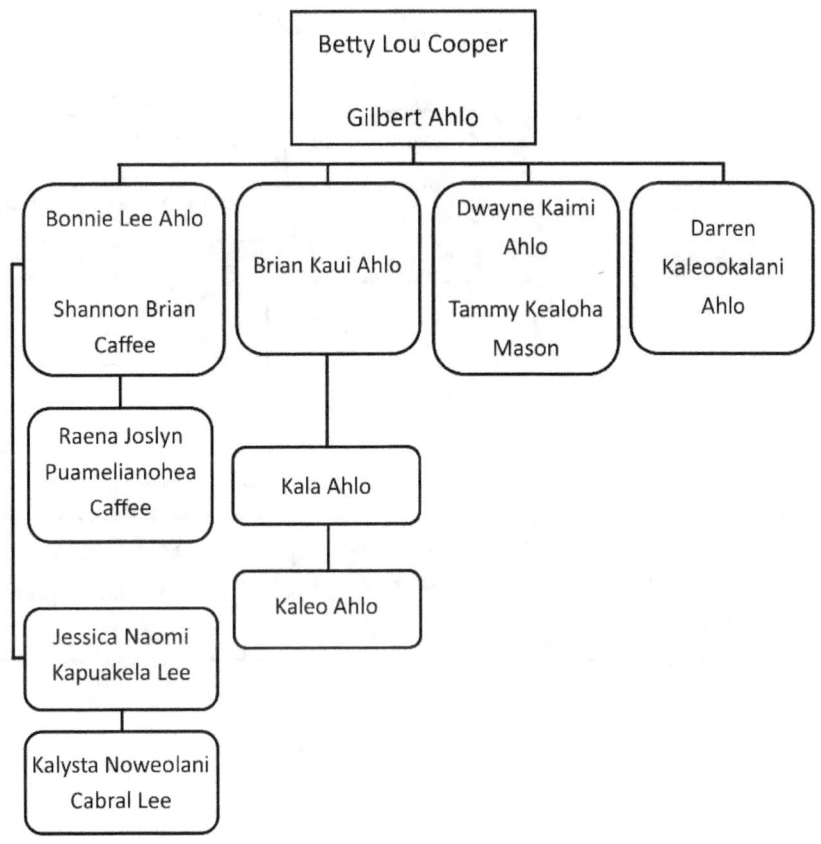

*Betty Lou passed away on 14 May 1992.
*Brian passed away in November 2016 and leaves two sons, Kala and Kaleo.
*Darren was killed in an automobile accident as a teenager
*Jessica's mother, Bonnie, never married; Jessica was raised principally by her Grandparents, Gilbert and Dolores, and oftentimes lived with my sister Judy Mae and Muts; Jessica now has a beautiful 3-year old daughter, Kalysta Noweolani.

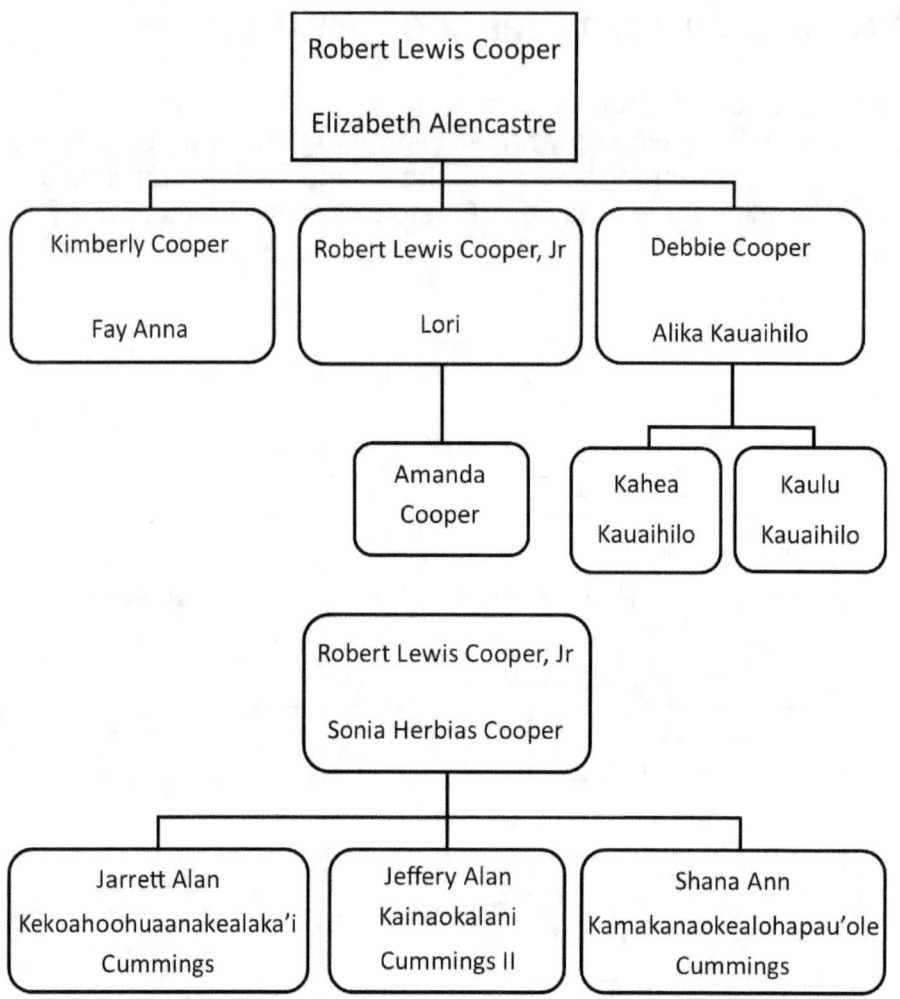

*Kawai married Lori, then divorced shortly after Amanda was born who was raised by Lori
*Kawai then married Sonia who together raised Sonia's three children

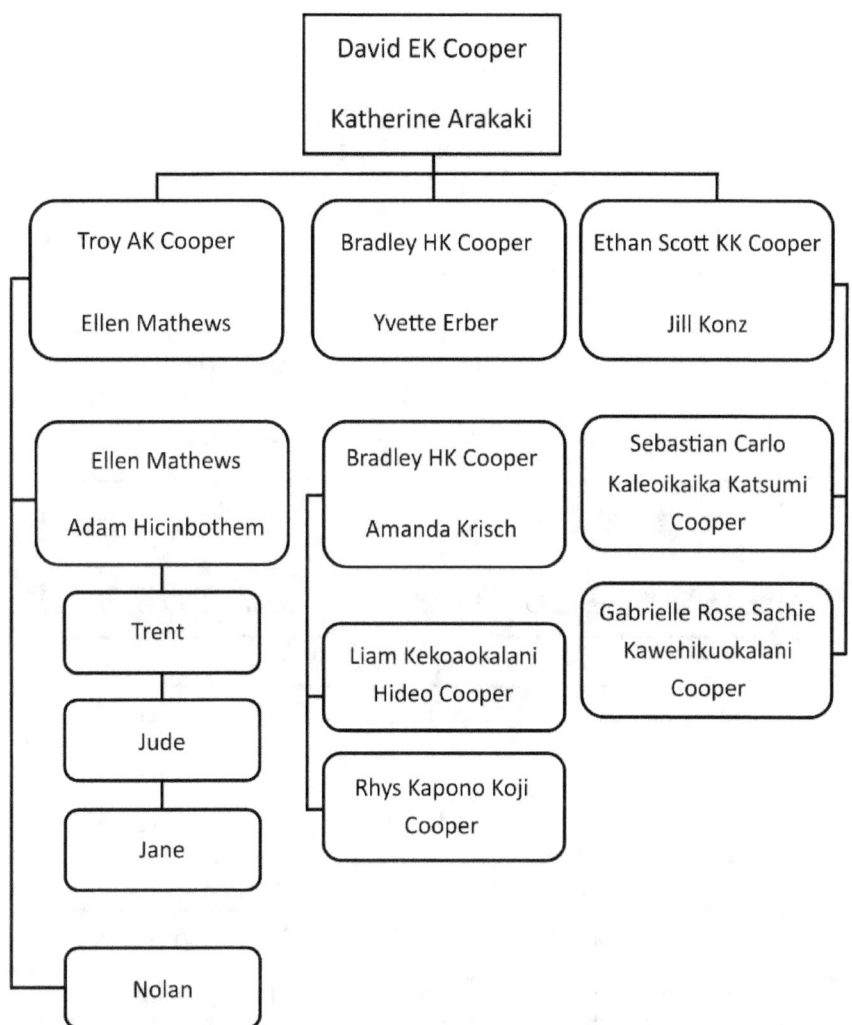

*Brad and Yvette were Temple Law School classmates, married but divorced several years later
*Ellen is the daughter of Ellen, married and has two boys and a daughter
*Nolan is the son of Ellen and expects to graduate in 2018 from Northwestern University
Troy and Ellen have no children of their own.

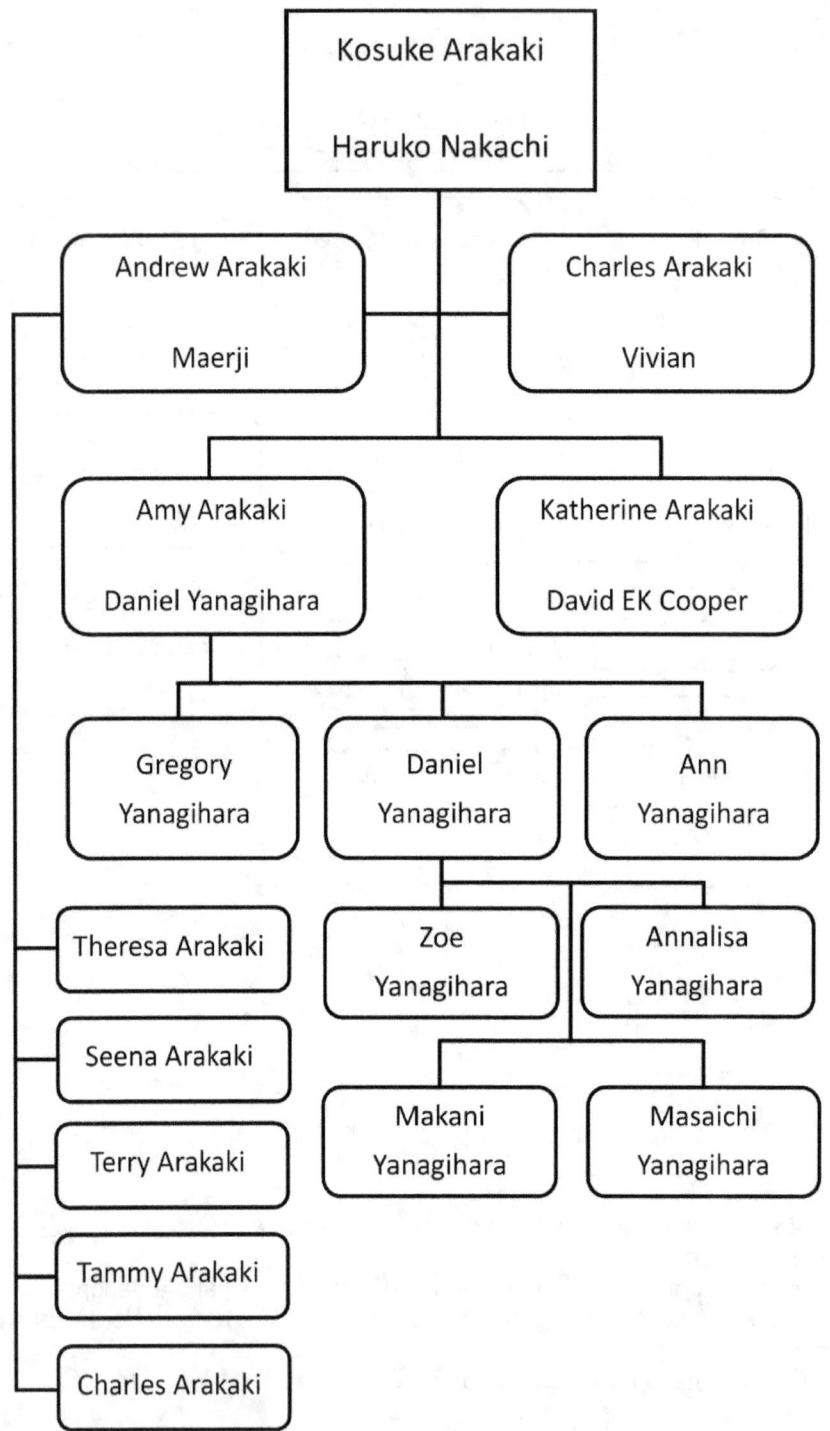

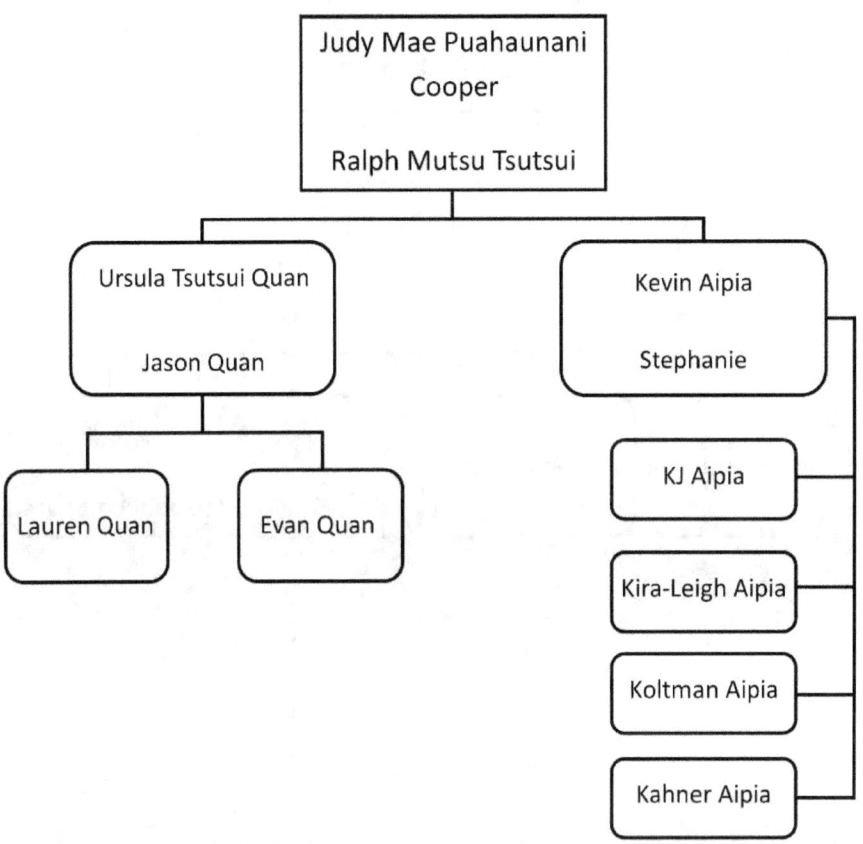

*Kevin is hanai brother to Ursula, and both were raised by Judy and Muts

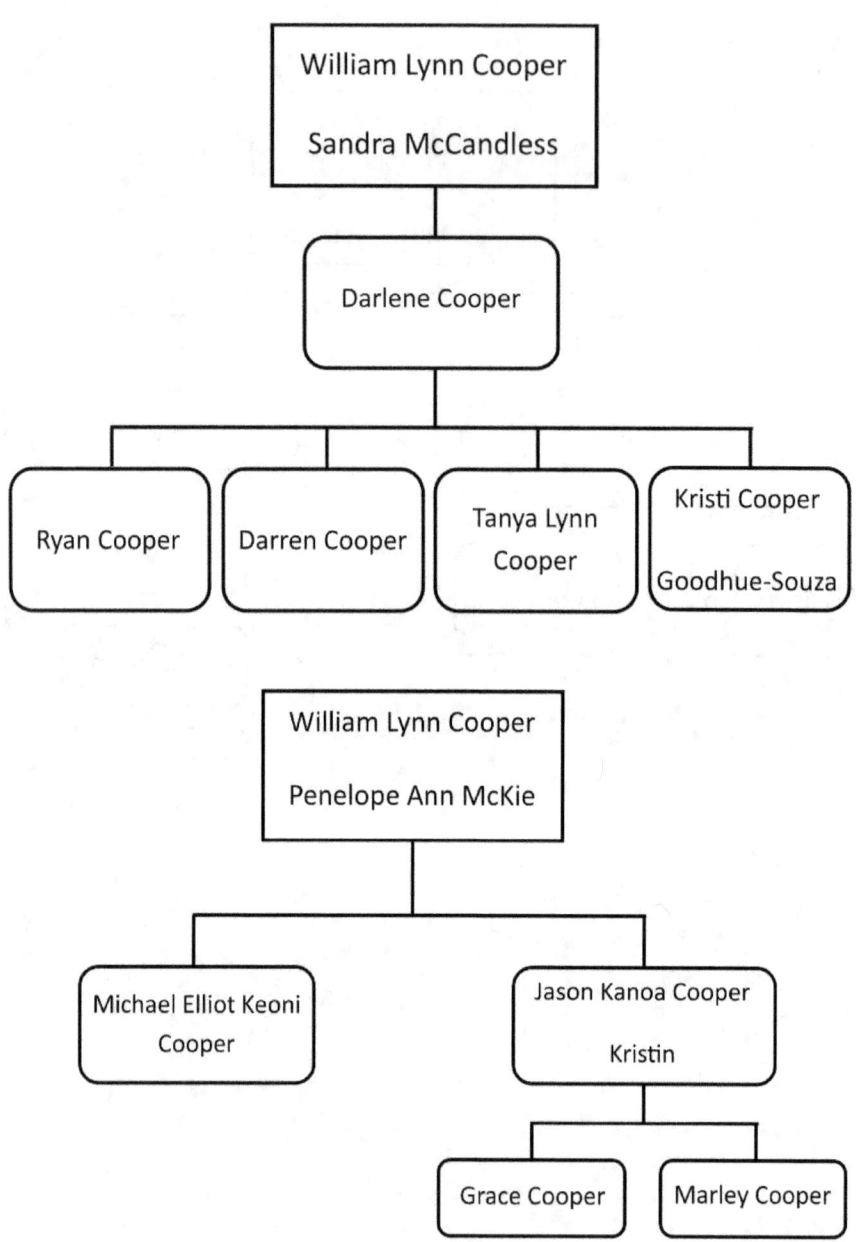

*Bill passed away on 5 December 2011.
*Jason and Kristin divorced in 2008; both have joint custody of the two girls.

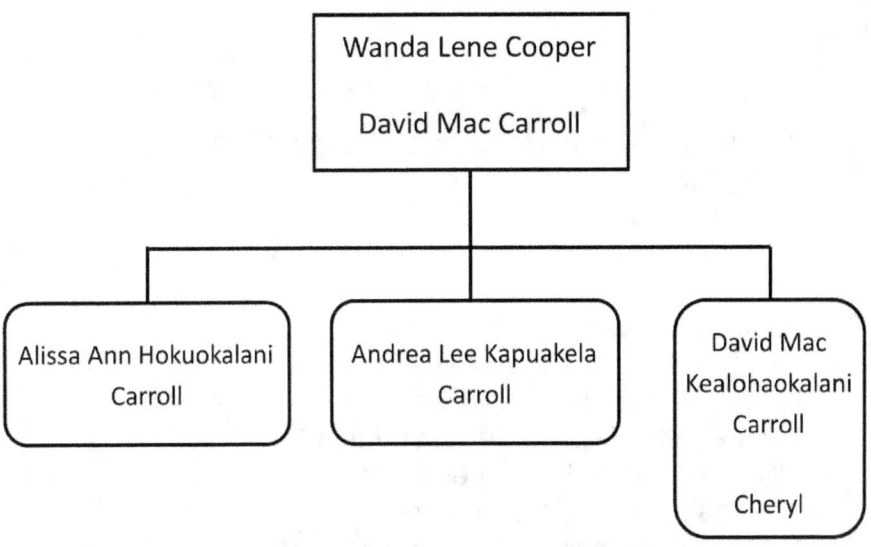

*Wanda passed away on 20 May 2002 and her ashes have not yet been laid to rest.

Bibliography

Adolpho, Julie K. Julie K. Adolpho's Groups: My Kamaka Family Tree; Maoliworld, 2017.

Ancestry, 1997-2017

    John K. Kamaka, Ancestry.com
    Charles K. Kamaka, Ancestry.com
    Joseph K. Kamaka, Ancestry.com
    Henrietta K. Kamaka, Ancestry.com
    William K. Kamaka, Ancestry.com
    Thelma K. Kamaka, Ancestry.com
    Ronald K. Kamaka, Ancestry.com
    Polly Kamaka, Ancestry.com
    Annie K. Kamaka, Ancestry.com
    Lucy K. Kamaka, Ancestry.com
    Daniel K. Kamaka, Ancestry.com
    Rachel K. Kamaka, Ancestry.com
    Abraham K. Kamaka, Ancestry.com
    Abraham K. Kamaka, World War II Army Enlistment Records, 1938-1946

Cataluna, Lee, Honolulu Star Advertiser, "A Villain Fans Loved to Hate," Sunday, August 19, 2007

Cooper, David EK. "The David Cooper Family Tree," Ancestry.com, 2016.

Dawson, Teresa. Environment Hawaii, Volume 13, Number 11, May 2003, "Marines' Plan for Jungle Training in Waikane Valley Reopens Old Wounds."

Hoe, Kelikokauaikekai R. "S.E.K. Papa'ai, A Study of the Survival of Maoli Beliefs in Mele of the Nineteenth Century," A Thesis Submitted to the Graduate Division of the University of Hawai'i in Partial Fulfillment of the Requirements for the Degree of Master of Arts in Religion; May 2004.

Honolulu Star Bulletin Obituaries, Article, Lucy Kapaeloa Cooper Notice of Death

Honolulu Star Advertiser Obituaries, Archive for September 16, 2016

Honolulu Star Advertiser Obituaries, Archive for December 30, 2016

Oregon Department of Human Resources, Health Division, Center for Health Statistics, Certificate of Death, Betty Lou K. Armstrong, May 14, 1992

U.S. Federal Census, 1930

U.S. Federal Census, 1940

U.S. Social Security Applications and Claims Index, 1935-2014

U.S. Social Security Applications and Claims Index, 1936-2007

U.S. Social Security Death Index, 1935-2014

Viotti, Vicki. Honolulu Star Advertiser. "Hiram Kamaka, State Budget Director, Dead at 76," Wednesday, January 7, 2004

Endnotes

Chapter 1. Genealogy

1. I have attempted to identify as accurately as possible the dates of birth and deaths, as well as their Hawaiian names, of all twelve of the Kamaka siblings; follow on research may provide more accurate dates. I listed each in the order of their birth, and as you can see from the dates of their deaths, the youngest, Daniel, died at age 13 and eldest, Aunty Ka'akau, died at age 91.

2. The genealogy for the period of birth and death of my Grandparents, Aunts and Uncles uses the distinctive word "About" simply because records were not appropriately kept; I found it especially interesting that my Grandfather's birth records cited either 1864 or 1877 or 1878; I selected 1877 as the most probable date of birth given the birth of Uncle John in 1898, a birth date that is fairly firm as that would have made my Grandfather's age at 21, rather than age 20 at a birth of 1978 or age 34 at a birth date of 1864.

3. Unfortunately my research has not yet determined an accurate date for the death of Uncle Abraham; so I used the term "About" and the year as 1982.

4. Uncle Daniel was a surprise as I heard that he had died at birth, not at age 13.

5. The Daniel P. Kaialau who is listed in the 1930 United States Federal Census Results with our genealogy was a boarder and not a family member. John Kuahilo, born about 1895, was a cousin.

6. Uncle William's birth is either 1904 or 1905; I chose 1904; his death is listed as either about 2004 or 1985; I chose 1985 based on the knowledge that Aunty Ka'akau's was the last Kamaka sibling to die in 1994.

7. I had always thought my brother's, William Lynn, or Bill, Hawaiian name, Kamakananahukilani, was the same as my Grandfather's; but my Grandfather's Hawaiian name was Kaoholowahi; Bill's Hawaiian name is the same as Uncle Ronald's, Kamakananahukilani. An interesting note is that my Great Grandfather's Hawaiian name was Kaohelowahi, slightly different than my Grandfather's Hawaiian name of Kaoholowahi.

8. I am not quite sure of Polly Kamaka, but she is listed in the 1940 United States Federal Census of our genealogy following Uncle Ronald and under her name is McRonald, age 3, and Raymond, with the date of 11/12, probably his birth date; I assume that she was the first wife of Uncle Ronald; hence, I have listed her as such.

9. The dates of birth and deaths of my twenty-seven first cousins have not been listed; but where I could, I did identify their Hawaiian names, spouses and the number of children. I have sent a draft copy to each family for verification of the names, dates, number of children, validation of the descriptive terms in the narrative and further specific examples they would like to see in this publication.

Chapter 2. Kingdom Days

1. It is an educated guess that my Grandfather was given all those parcels of land for service to the Kingdom; while there is no evidence of an official decree assigning those parcels of land to my Grandfather, I recall sufficient stories by my Aunts and Mother that Grandfather exercised common law ownership of most of the land, including the property at 321 North Kuakini Street; as to the family's 3-acres in Waikane, my inference is that it came with the authorities granted to the Native Hawaiians as part of the Great Mahele of 1848.

2. While my parents prepared their 12,000 square feet of apportioned land in Waikane over a 2-year period, we lived in a 7-bedroom home, one bathroom, a kitchen, one flush

toilet, and a 3-party telephone line with Aunty Thelma's and Aunty Rachel's families, a total of 19-20 people, including our family; we never argued, nor found things about which to complain; the first to move into their new home in Waikane was Aunty Thelma's family, followed by us and finally Aunty Rachel's family. The property and home at 321 North Kuakini Street was sold and eventually torn down for Kuakini Hospital's parking lot.

3. Betty Lou, Sonny and I attended Kauluwela Elementary School through the sixth grade; Betty Lou then entered Kawananakoa Intermediate School until she was accepted by Kamehameha School for Girls starting her 10th grade year; Sonny and I both entered Kamehameha School for Boys in our 7th grade year. Judy Mae lived with Aunty Ka'akau and Uncle Willie at their home in Waikane, attended Waiahole Elementary School until she entered Kamehameha School for Girls in her 7th grade year.

4. It is historically interesting that the home at 321 North Kuakini Street had a flush toilet, Aunty Ka'akau and Uncle Willie's home in Waikane used an outhouse until probably 1956.

5. The 187 acres in Waikane Valley that was stolen continue to haunt my entire generation of Kamakas; that Judge Sam King, a Native Hawaiian, could have ruled against the Kamaka family on grounds that deny the technological advances in land remediation of that time, as well as the Navy's ruling nearly the same time to spend nearly $350M in the unexploded ordnance removal at Kaho'olawe, defies logic, especially the fact that there can be no more land growth on an island as Oahu. It has been nearly 33 years since the land was condemned based on Eminent Domain; it is time to return the land to the Kamaka family.

Chapter 3. Territory, State and Modern Hawaii

1. Every Kamaka family had its heroes and heroines; those who entered the mainstream of our country did so because of their personal drive and competitive spirit; those who did not were unable to break through the ceiling of institutional and quiet, pernicious biases focused on Americans who did not look like the European settlers of our country.

2. In Hawai'i, all non-white races suffered from discrimination and most out-whited the whites, so to speak, but most Native Hawaiians were unable to pull themselves up from the economic, governance, educational, social and healthcare status of mediocrity in which they were positioned.

3. Educational programs and academic institutions, like Kamehameha Schools, did much to change the environment; but it was Native Hawaiian leaders, joined by others, who stood for what is right and *pono* (just) who brought hope to the element of change.

Chapters 4-12. The Kamaka Family

As I mentioned in my Foreword, I trust the narrative of my recollections ring true to my Kamaka family.

Chapter 13. The Modern Kamaka Ohana – The Challenges

1. The transition from my Mother's generation to our generation was not without real challenges; my generation moved the needle to the right of center, defining the issues, educating emerging leaders, leading protests in the streets and recognizing that public policies do make a real difference.

2. But it is our children's generation, the next generation of Kamakas, that real progress can and must be made to preserving Native Hawaiians, their culture, language, traditions and societal values.

3. In my view, the path to preservation must be through learning that starts in early childhood and continues through higher education; economic strength through successful businesses; full involvement in the public policy process including the US Congress and our Hawaii State Legislature; establishing Political Action Committees to educate and inform policymakers on environment, healthcare, education and housing issues; participating in community development; and involvement in leadership mentoring programs, among other initiatives.

4. A particular nagging issue is the attitude of some Native Hawaiians that somehow some are more Native Hawaiian than other Native Hawaiians, especially those living on the mainland who today represent about 49%of the more than 575,000 Native Hawaiians in our country. It has been called the 200% syndrome.

5. Every Native Hawaiian is critical to our preservation; should we somehow rally around a Native Hawaiian or other leader who provides the hope we are all seeking, and forego the constant arguments that divide us rather than unite us, as the experiences I witnessed during the Kamaka family discussions Saturday evenings at my parents Waikane home, then there can be a critical path that leads to full participation as respected and honorable citizens in our State and country.

References

ancestry

All 1930 United States Federal Census Results

Provided in association with National Archives and Records Administration

Search Filters Filters First

Edit Search   New Search

All Categories
> Census & Voter Lists
> 1930s

1930 United States Federal Census

The 1930 Census contains records for approximately 123 million Americans. The census gives us a glimpse into the lives of Americans in 1930, and contains information about a household's family...

Learn more about this database...

Browse Individual Records ▸

Shortcut Keys ▸

To get better results, add more information such as **First Name, Last Name, Birth Info, Death Info or Location**—even a guess will help. Edit your search or learn more.

View Record	Name	Parent or spouse names	Home in 1930 (City, County, State)	Birth Year	Birthplace	Relation to Head of House	View Image
View Record	John Kamaka	Annie	Koolaupoko, Honolulu, Hawaii Territory	abt 1878	Hawaii	Head	
View Record	Annie Kamaka	John	Koolaupoko, Honolulu, Hawaii Territory	abt 1880	Hawaii	Wife	
View Record	John K Kamaka	John, Annie	Koolaupoko, Honolulu, Hawaii Territory	abt 1900	Hawaii	Son	
View Record	Charles M Kamaka	John, Annie	Koolaupoko, Honolulu, Hawaii Territory	abt 1901	Hawaii	Son	
View Record	Henrietta Kamaka	John, Annie	Koolaupoko, Honolulu, Hawaii Territory	abt 1903	Hawaii	Daughter	
View Record	William K Kamaka	John, Annie	Koolaupoko, Honolulu, Hawaii Territory	abt 1905	Hawaii	Son	
View Record	Joseph K Kamaka	John, Annie	Koolaupoko, Honolulu, Hawaii Territory	abt 1907	Hawaii	Son	
View Record	Ronald L Kamaka		Koolaupoko, Honolulu, Hawaii Territory	abt 1909	Hawaii	Son	
View Record	Thelma K Kamaka	John, Annie	Koolaupoko, Honolulu, Hawaii Territory	abt 1912	Hawaii	Daughter	

	Name	Related	Location	Birth	Birthplace	Relationship	
View Record	Lucy K Kamaka	John, Annie	Koolaupoko, Honolulu, Hawaii Territory	abt 1914	Hawaii	Daughter	
View Record	Rachel H Kamaka	John, Annie	Koolaupoko, Honolulu, Hawaii Territory	abt 1917	Hawaii	Daughter	
View Record	Abraham K Kamaka	John, Annie	Koolaupoko, Honolulu, Hawaii Territory	abt 1921	Hawaii	Son	
View Record	Alfred K Morita	Annie K	Koolaupoko, Honolulu, Hawaii Territory	abt 1907	Hawaii	Son-in-law	
View Record	Annie K Morita	John, Annie, Alfred K	Koolaupoko, Honolulu, Hawaii Territory	abt 1910	Hawaii	Daughter	
View Record	Alfred K Morita	Alfred K, Annie K	Koolaupoko, Honolulu, Hawaii Territory	abt 1928	Hawaii	Grandson	
View Record	John K Kuahlio		Koolaupoko, Honolulu, Hawaii Territory	abt 1895	Hawaii	Cousin	
View Record	Daniel P Kalalau		Koolaupoko, Honolulu, Hawaii Territory	abt 1895	Hawaii	Boarder	
View Record	Choho Zukilan	Oto	Koolaupoko, Honolulu, Hawaii Territory	abt 1888	Japan	Head	
View Record	Oto Zukilan	Choho	Koolaupoko, Honolulu, Hawaii Territory	abt 1890	Japan	Wife	
View Record	Kichi Zukilan	Choho, Oto	Koolaupoko, Honolulu, Hawaii Territory	abt 1915	Hawaii	Son	
View Record	Choso Zukilan	Choho, Oto	Koolaupoko, Honolulu, Hawaii Territory	abt 1919	Hawaii	Son	
View Record	Asao Zukilan	Choho, Oto	Koolaupoko, Honolulu, Hawaii Territory	abt 1924	Hawaii	Son	
View Record	Choio Zukilan	Choho, Oto	Koolaupoko, Honolulu, Hawaii Territory	abt 1927	Hawaii	Son	

View Record	Asako Zukitan	Choho, Oto	Koolaupoko, Honolulu, Hawaii Territory	abt 1930	Hawaii	Daughter	
View Record	William K Pahia		Koolaupoko, Honolulu, Hawaii Territory	abt 1902	Hawaii	Head	
View Record	Lily W Pahia	William K	Koolaupoko, Honolulu, Hawaii Territory	abt 1927	Hawaii	Daughter	
View Record	Imon Murakami	Hisa	Koolaupoko, Honolulu, Hawaii Territory	abt 1875	Japan	Head	
View Record	Hisa Murakami	Imon	Koolaupoko, Honolulu, Hawaii Territory	abt 1890	Japan	Wife	
View Record	Toyozo Nakajo		Koolaupoko, Honolulu, Hawaii Territory	abt 1860	Japan	Head	
View Record	Riosaku Sato		Koolaupoko, Honolulu, Hawaii Territory	abt 1867	Japan	Head	
View Record	Watanabe Kianosuki		Koolaupoko, Honolulu, Hawaii Territory	abt 1876	Japan	Head	
View Record	Togoichi Shiratori	Monshido, Hisako	Koolaupoko, Honolulu, Hawaii Territory	abt 1898	Japan	Head	
View Record	Hisako Shiratori	Togoichi	Koolaupoko, Honolulu, Hawaii Territory	abt 1905	Hawaii	Wife	
View Record	Fugio Shiratori	Togoichi, Hisako	Koolaupoko, Honolulu, Hawaii Territory	abt 1927	Hawaii	Son	
View Record	Tochio Shiratori	Togoichi, Hisako	Koolaupoko, Honolulu, Hawaii Territory	abt 1928	Hawaii	Son	
View Record	Monshido Shiratori		Koolaupoko, Honolulu, Hawaii Territory	abt 1873	Japan	Father	
View Record	Edward K Haleakala	Mary	Koolaupoko, Honolulu, Hawaii Territory	abt 1873	Hawaii	Head	

ancestry

All results for Annie Kamaka

Search Filters Filters Reset   Exact

Annie

Kamaka

BORN 1910

ANY Waikane, Ho...

COLLECTION   All Collections

Edit Search   New Search

RESULTS

All Categories

> Census & Voter Lists   1,104

> Birth, Marriage & Death   1,092

> Military   106

> Immigration & Travel   410

  Newspapers &   277
  Publications

  Pictures   36

> Stories, Memories &   79
  Histories

  Maps, Atlases &   2
  Gazetteers

> Schools, Directories &   >5,000
  Church Histories

> Wills, Probates, Land,   387
  Tax & Criminal

  Reference, Dictionaries &   1
  Almanacs

  Family Trees   1,557

Shortcut Keys +

Results 1–20 of 14,341

Matching Person (from family trees)

See more like this ...

Birth: Abt 1910
Death: 1993 - Honolulu, HI (Hawaii)
Parents: John Kaoholowahi
Kamaka, Annie Kahonuasuioka'u Hatton

Annie K Kamaka
KAMAKA Family tree

Matching Records

1930 United States Federal Census
CENSUS & VOTER LISTS
View Image

NAME Annie K Morita
SPOUSE Alfred K Morita
BIRTH abt 1910 - Hawaii
RESIDENCE 1930 - Koolaupoko, Honolulu, Hawaii Territory

1940 United States Federal Census
CENSUS & VOTER LISTS
View Image

NAME Annie T Kamaka
SPOUSE William Kamaka
BIRTH abt 1907 - Hawaii
RESIDENCE 1935
RESIDENCE Koolaupoko, Honolulu, Hawaii

1930 United States Federal Census
CENSUS & VOTER LISTS
View Image

NAME Annie Blockwood
SPOUSE Loarn E Blockwood
BIRTH abt 1913 - Hawaii
RESIDENCE 1930 - Honolulu, Honolulu, Hawaii Territory

U.S., Social Security Death Index,
1935-2014
BIRTH, MARRIAGE & DEATH

NAME Annie T. Kamaka
BIRTH 20 Aug 1906
DEATH 29 Aug 1987 - Kaneohe, Honolulu, Hawaii, USA
LAST Hawaii

Public Member Photos & Scanned
Documents
PICTURES

PHOTO Raymond Judd & Annie Kamaka
CATEGORY Other

RECORDS   CATEGORIES

ancestry

All Public Member Trees results for Annie Kamaka

Search Filters Filter Road   Enci

Annie

Kamaka

BORN 1910

Are Waikane, Ho...

COLLECTION   All Collections

Edit Search   New Search

Family Trees

Public Member Trees

This database contains family trees submitted to Ancestry by users who have indicated that their tree can be viewed by all Ancestry subscribers. These trees can change over time as users edit,...

Learn more about this database...

Shortcut Keys ▸

Results 1–1 of 1

Member Tree	Name	Parents
KAMAKA Family Tree	Annie K Kamaka	F: John Kaoholowahi Kamaka
Public Member Tree 2 attached records, 3 sources	Birth: Abt 1910 Death: 1993 - Honolulu, HI (Hawaii)	M: Annie Kahonuanuioka'u Hatton

1–1 of 1

Per page   20

ancestry

Annie K Morita
in the 1930 United States Federal Census

📄 View blank form

✎ Add alternate information

⚠ Report issue

Name	Annie K Morita [Annie K Kamaka]
Birth Year	abt 1910
Gender	Female
Race	Hawaiian
Birthplace	Hawaii
Marital Status	Married
Relation to Head of House	Daughter
Home in 1930	Koolaupoko, Honolulu, Hawaii Territory
Map of Home	View Map
Able to Read and Write	No
Father's Birthplace	Hawaii
Mother's Birthplace	Hawaii

Household Members: Name	Age
John Kamaka	52
Annie Kamaka	50
John K Kamaka	30
Charles M Kamaka	29
Henrietta Kamaka	27
William K Kamaka	25
Joseph K Kamaka	23
Ronald L Kamaka	21
Thelma K Kamaka	18
Lucy K Kamaka	16
	13

Provided in association with National Archives and Records Administration

Suggested Records

📄 1940 United States Federal Census
Annie K Morita

📄 1920 United States Federal Census
Hannah Kamaka

📄 U.S., Social Security Death Index, 1935-2014
Annie Kamaka

Write a comment

Make a Connection

Find others who are researching Annie K Morita in Public Member Trees

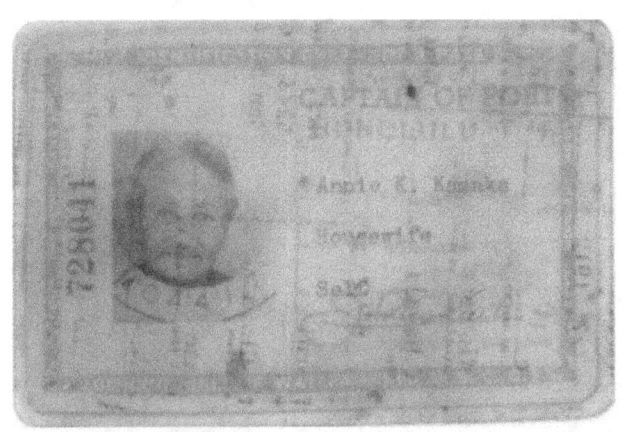

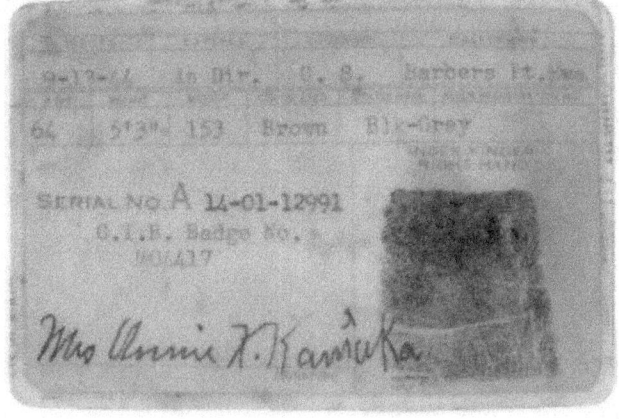

ancestry

John Kamaka
in the 1930 United States Federal Census

🔲 View blank form

✎ Add alternate information

⚠ Report issue

Name:	John Kamaka
Birth Year:	abt 1878
Gender:	Male
Race:	Hawaiian
Birthplace:	Hawaii
Marital Status:	Married
Relation to Head of House:	Head
Home in 1930:	Koolaupoko, Honolulu, Hawaii Territory
Map of Home:	View Map
Radio Set:	No
Able to Read and Write:	No
Father's Birthplace:	Hawaii
Mother's Birthplace:	Hawaii

Household Members	Name	Age
	John Kamaka	52
	Annie Kamaka	50
	John K Kamaka	30
	Charles M Kamaka	29
	Henrietta Kamaka	27
	William K Kamaka	25
	Joseph K Kamaka	23
	Ronald L Kamaka	21
	Thelma K Kamaka	18
	Lucy K Kamaka	16

Provided in association with National Archives and Records Administration

Suggested Records ❓

🔲 1920 United States Federal Census
John Kamaka

🔲 1940 United States Federal Census
Joseph Kamakea

🔲 1920 United States Federal Census
Jose Kamacis

🔲 U.S., Find A Grave Index, 1600s-Current
Joseph Namea Kamakea

🔲 1900 United States Federal Census
Kamaka

🔲 U.S. City Directories, 1822-1995
John Kamaka

Show More ⌄

Write a comment

Make a Connection

Find others who are researching John Kamaka in Public Member Trees

Name	Age
Rachel H Kamaka	13
Abraham K Kamaka	9
Alfred K Morita	23
Annie K Morita	20
Alfred K Morita	2
John K Kuahilo	35
Daniel P Kalalau	35

Neighbors: View others on page

SAVE ∨   Cancel

Source Citation

Year: 1930; Census Place: Koolaupoko, Honolulu, Hawaii Territory; Roll: 2636, Page: 28; Enumeration District: 0123; Image: 115.0; FHL microfilm: 2342370

Source Information

Ancestry.com. 1930 United States Federal Census [database on-line]. Provo, UT, USA: Ancestry.com Operations Inc., 2002.

Original data: United States of America, Bureau of the Census. Fifteenth Census of the United States, 1930. Washington, D.C.: National Archives and Records Administration, 1930. T626, 2,667 rolls.

Description

The 1930 Census contains records for approximately 123 million Americans. The census gives us a glimpse into the lives of Americans in 1930, and contains information about a household's family members and occupants including: birthplaces, occupations, immigration, citizenship, and military service. The names of those listed in the census are linked to actual images of the 1930 Census. Learn more...

ancestry

All Public Member Trees results for John Kamaka

John

Kamaka

born 1877

Edit Search   New Search

Family Trees

Public Member Trees

This database contains family trees submitted to Ancestry by users who have indicated that their tree can be viewed by all Ancestry subscribers. These trees can change over time as users edit,...

Learn more about this database...

Shortcut Keys »

Results 1–20 of 738

Member Tree	Name	Parents
Molly Olson family tree Public Member Tree 1 attached record, 2 sources	John Kamaka Birth: 14 Jan. 1877 Death: 6 Jan 1936 - Honolulu, HI (Hawaii) Spouse: Ane Kahonuanuioka'u Aalona Hatton	F: (Name Unknown) M: (Name Unknown)
KAMAKA Family Tree Public Member Tree 1 attached record, 2 sources	John Kaoholowahi Kamaka Birth: 14 Jan 1877 - Oahu (Honolulu), USA Death: 6 Jan 1936 - Honolulu, Hawaii, United States Spouse: Annie Kahonuanuioka'u Hatton	F: (Name Unknown) M: (Name Unknown)
KAMAKA Family Tree Public Member Tree 1 source	John Kaoholowahi Kamaka Birth: 14 Jan 1877 - Oahu (Honolulu), USA Death: 6 Jan 1936 - Honolulu, Hawaii, United States	F: (Name Unknown) M: (Name Unknown)
Sorensen Fitzgerald Public Member Tree 1 attached record, 2 sources	John Kaoholowahi or Kaoheloahi Kamaka Birth: 14 Jan 1877 - Oahu (Honolulu), USA Death: 6 Jan 1936 - Honolulu, Hawaii, United States Spouse: Ane Kahonuanuioka'u Aalona Hatton	F: Joseph Kaoheloahi Kamaka M: (Name Unknown)
Kamaka Family Tree Public Member Tree 2 attached records, 3 sources	John Kaoholowahi Kamaka Birth: 14 Jan. 1877 Death: 6 Jan 1936 - Honolulu, HI (Hawaii) Spouse: Ane Kahonuanuioka'u Aalona Hatton	F: Joseph Kaoheloahi Kamaka M: (Name Unknown)
Kamaka Family Tree Public Member	John Kaoholowahi Kamaka Birth: 14 Jan 1877 - Oahu (Honolulu), USA Death: 6 Jan 1936 - Honolulu,	F: Joseph Kaoheloahi Kamaka M: (Name Unknown)

Tree   Hawaii, United States
1 source   Spouse: Annie Kahonuanuioka'u Hatton

BDisque

Public Member Tree
1 attached record, 2 sources

John Kamaka

Birth: Abt 1878
Spouse: Kawai Maa

F: (Name Unknown)
M: (Name Unknown)

Catryna Griep family tree

Public Member Tree
4 attached records, 5 sources & photos

John Kaoholowahi Kamaka

Birth: 1878 - Honolulu
Death: Honolulu, Honolulu, Hawaii Territory (Hawaii)
Spouse: Ane Kahonuanuioka'u Aalona Hatton

F: (Name Unknown)
M: (Name Unknown)

Adolpho Family Tree

Public Member Tree
1 attached record, 1 source

John K. Kamaka

Birth: Abt 1878
Spouse: Annie Hatton

F: (Name Unknown)
M: (Name Unknown)

Nicole Yogi Family Tree

Public Member Tree
1 attached record, 1 source

John Kamaka

Birth: Abt 1878
Spouse: Annie Aalona Hatton

F: (Name Unknown)
M: (Name Unknown)

Ipo Dahl's Family Tree

Public Member Tree
5 attached records, 5 sources

Makaio aka John Kamaka

Birth: 1875
Marriage: Sep 1910 - Hawaiian (Hawaii)
Spouse: Mary or May Keahonua Hanamaikai

F: Kahinu
M: Neneue

David Cooper family tree

Public Member Tree
1 attached record, 1 source

John Kamaka

Birth: About 1880 - Honolulu, USA
Death: About 1950 - Honolulu, Honolulu, Hawaii, USA
Spouse: Annie Hatton

F: (Name Unknown)
M: (Name Unknown)

McMillon Research Tree *

Public Member Tree
1 attached

John Kamaka

Birth: Jan 1882

F: (Name Unknown)
M: Kamaka

record, 1
source

Carroll Family
Tree

Public Member
Tree
1 source

John Kaoholowahi Kamaka

F: (Name
Unknown)
M: (Name
Unknown)

Christner Family
Tree

Public Member
Tree
15 attached
records, 15
sources &
photos

John Kinik

Birth: 18 Jan 1877 - Hungary
Death: 21 Feb 1961 - Belle Vernon,
Pennsylvania, USA
Spouse: Julianna Koncz

F: Kinik

M: (Name
Unknown)

Young Family
Tree

Public Member
Tree
1 source

JOHN NEWTON aka IONE NUTIN
NUKUNA Kameekua

Birth: 12 Feb 1877
Death: 08oct1917 (8 Oct 1917) -
Honolulu, Honolulu, Hawaii, USA
Marriage: 13 Feb 1904 - Honolulu,
Hawaii
Spouse: Esther Ekekela
Keliikahiole Nakea

F: Newton
"Nukuna"
Kameekua
M: Kaili'ohe
Pe'elua

Sandy (Villwock)
Young Family -4

Public Member
Tree
1 attached
record, 4
sources

JOHN NEWTON aka IONE NUTIN
NUKUNA Kameekua

Birth: 12 Feb 1877
Death: 08 Oct 1917 (8 Oct 1917) -
Honolulu, Hawaii
Marriage: 13 Feb 1904 - Honolulu,
Hawaii
Spouse: Esther Ekekela
Keliikahiole Nakea

F: Newton
"Nukuna"
Kameekua
M: Kaili'ohe
Pe'elua

Bybee-Maddox
Tree of hugeness

Public Member
Tree
3 sources

John Kimmich

Birth: 25 Jun 1877
Marriage: 3 Jul 1897
Spouse: Frances Elizabeth Metzler

F: George
Kimmich
M: Christine Grove

Vatter III Family
Tree

Public Member
Tree
1 source

John Kimmich

Birth: 25 Jun 1877 - United States

F: Johann Georg
Kimmich
M: Christiana
Herman

Reidenbaugh
Family Tree

Public Member
Tree
9 attached
records, 9
sources

John G. Kimmich

Birth: 25 Jun 1877
Marriage: 1898
Spouse: Francis Metzler

F: (Name
Unknown)
M: (Name
Unknown)

ancestry

Charles Kamaka

in the 1940 United States Federal Census

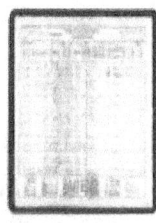

📄 View blank form

✏️ Add alternate information

⚠️ Report issue

Name:	Charles Kamaka
Age:	40
Estimated birth year:	abt 1900
Gender:	Male
Race:	Part-Hawaiian (Hawaiian)
Birthplace:	Hawaii
Marital Status:	Single
Relation to Head of House:	Son
Home in 1940:	Koolaupoko, Honolulu, Hawaii
Map of Home in 1940:	View Map
Street:	Kamehameha Highway
Sheet Number:	5B
Occupation:	Cantonnier
Attended School or College:	No
Highest Grade Completed:	Elementary school, 3rd grade
Hours Worked Week Prior to Census:	45
Class of Worker:	Wage or salary worker
Weeks Worked in 1939:	52
Income:	900
Income Other Sources:	No
Neighbors:	View others on page

Household Members	Name	Age
	Annie Kamaka	54
	Charles Kamaka	40
	Joseph Kamaka	34

Provided in association with National Archives and Records Administration

Suggested Records ❓

📄 1930 United States Federal Census
Charles M Kamaka

📄 1930 United States Federal Census
John K Kamaka

📄 California, Death Index, 1940-1997
Charles Kamaka

📄 U.S., Social Security Death Index, 1935-2014
Charles Kamaka

Write a comment.

Make a Connection

Find others who are researching Charles Kamaka in Public Member Trees

ancestry

Charles Kamaka
in the U.S., Social Security Death Index, 1935-2014

No Image

Request copy of
original application

Add alternate
information

Report issue

Name:	Charles Kamaka
SSN:	575-40-4114
Last Residence:	96817 Honolulu, Honolulu, Hawaii, USA
Born:	31 Dec 1900
Died:	Jan 1968
State (Year) SSN Issued:	Hawaii (1957-1958)

SAVE Cancel

Suggested Records

1930 United States Federal Census
Charles M Kamaka

1940 United States Federal Census
Charles Kamaka

Write a comment

Source Citation
Number: *575-40-4114*; Issue State: *Hawaii*; Issue Date: *1957-1958*

Source Information
Ancestry.com. U.S., *Social Security Death Index, 1935-2014* [database on-line]. Provo, UT, USA: Ancestry.com Operations Inc, 2011.

Original data: Social Security Administration. *Social Security Death Index, Master File*. Social Security Administration.

Description
The Social Security Administration Death Master File contains information on millions of deceased individuals with United States social security numbers whose deaths were reported to the Social Security Administration. Birth years for the individuals listed range from 1875 to last year. Information in these records includes name, birth date, death date, and last known residence. Learn more...

Make a Connection
Find others who are researching Charles Kamaka in Public Member Trees

© 1997-2017 Ancestry

■ **Henrietta Kaakaualani Kamaka Pahia,** 94, of Kaneohe died Aug. 9 at home. Born in Waikane Koolaupoko, she is survived by children Joann Mersberg, Mary Aipia, Lily Galdeira and Hattie Lederer; and hanai children McRonald K. Kamaka, Kevin K. Aipia and Judy M.P. Tsutsui. Services: 12:30 p.m. tomorrow at Hawaiian Memorial Park Mortuary. Call after 10 a.m. Burial: Hawaiian Memorial Park. Casual attire.

■ **Marryat F. "Mickey" Parker Jr.,** 76, of Silverdale, Wash. and formerly of Honolulu, died July 10 at home. He served in the Navy during World War II and was chairman of Americal. Born in Berkeley, Calif., he is survived by wife Norma; sons Martin, David, John, Robert and Ron; daughter Rebecca; 10 grandchildren; and a great-grandchild. Memorial services: 11 a.m. tomorrow at Waiokeola Congregational Church, 4705 Kilauea Ave. Donations suggested to Hospice of Kitsap County, 3505 NW Anderson Hill Road, No. 208, Silverdale, WA 98383 or Waiokeola Congregational Church.

■ **Elmer D.R. Phillips,** 76, of Kailua, an architect, died Tuesday in Castle Hospital. He worked with Law & Wilson; Rothwell, Lester & Phillips; and Chapman Desai Sakata. Born in Bridgeville, Pa., he is survived by son Greg K.; daughter Abbie K. and Alison L.; brother William; and four grandchildren. Memorial services: 10 a.m. Monday at Faith Baptist Church, 1230 Kailua Road. Call after 9:30 a.m. Aloha attire. No flowers.

■ **Rosalio M. Reyes,** 58, of Kailua, past president of Honolulu Aerie No. 140 Fraternal Order of Eagles, died last Friday in Castle Hospital. Born in Lahaina, she is survived by mother Kathleen T. Orni; daughters Laura Lynn, Deanna Lauren and Leah M. Reyes; brothers Platon, Stanley, Walter, Wallace and William; sisters Margaret Tavares, Sandra Pavao and Grace Rico; and companion Marie McCabe. Services: 7 p.m. Monday at St. John Vianney Church. Call 6-9 p.m. Mass: 9:30 a.m. Tuesday at the church. Call after 9 a.m. Burial: Hawaii State Veterans Cemetery. Casual attire. No flowers.

■ **Rudy G. Saladino,** 56, of Mililani died Aug. 6 in Queen's Hospital. Born in Dingras, Ilocos Norte, the Philippines, he is survived by wife Erlinda C. "Linda"; son Joel-Adrian C.; mother Pacita G.; brothers Tim and Andrew; sister Alicia Tamayo; and father and mother-in-law Jaime and Guillerma Camba. Wake: 7 p.m. Sunday at Mililani Mortuary-Waipio, mauka chapel. Call 6-9 p.m. Mass: 9:30 a.m. Monday at Our Lady of Sorrows Church, 1403 California Ave., Wahiawa. Call after 8:30 a.m. Burial: Mililani Memorial Park. Casual attire.

■ **Takeo Sanpei,** 93, of Aiea, the retired owner of Sanpei Auto Service Station, died Saturday in Kapiolani Hospital at Pali Momi. Born in Fukushima, Japan, he is survived by wife Alice C.; sons Charles H., Francis T. and Edward M.; daughters Ellen F. Wakabayashi and Shirley C. Fujimoto; 11 grandchildren; and seven great-grandchildren. Private services.

■ **Kazuji Yasumiishi,** 89, of Honolulu, a retiree of S.H. Kress Co., died April 24 in Portland, Ore. Born in Honolulu, he is survived by son Calvin K.; four grandchildren; and two great-grandchildren. Graveside services over ashes: 9:30 a.m. Tuesday at Diamond Head Memorial Park. Casual attire. No flowers.

ancestry

William K Kamaka
in the 1930 United States Federal Census

📄 View blank form

✏ Add alternate information

⚠ Report issue

Name	William K Kamaka
Birth Year	abt 1905
Gender	Male
Race	Hawaiian
Birthplace	Hawaii
Marital Status	Single
Relation to Head of House	Son
Home in 1930	Koolaupoko, Honolulu, Hawaii Territory
Map of Home	View Map
Able to Read and Write	No
Father's Birthplace	Hawaii
Mother's Birthplace	Hawaii

Household Members	Name	Age
	John Kamaka	52
	Annie Kamaka	50
	John K Kamaka	30
	Charles M Kamaka	29
	Henrietta Kamaka	27
	William K Kamaka	25
	Joseph K Kamaka	23
	Ronald L Kamaka	21
	Thelma K Kamaka	18
	Lucy K Kamaka	16
	Rachel H Kamaka	13

Provided in association with National Archives and Records Administration

Suggested Records

📄 1910 United States Federal Census
Samuel Kamaka

📄 1940 United States Federal Census
William Kamaka

📄 1930 United States Federal Census
William Kamaka

📄 1930 United States Federal Census
William Kamakea

Write a comment.

Make a Connection

Find others who are researching William K Kamaka in Public Member Trees

ancestry

William Kamaka
in the U.S., Social Security Death Index, 1935-2014

No Image
Text only transcription

Request copy of
original application

Add alternate
information

Report issue

Name: William Kamaka

SSN: 575-05-6395

Last Residence: 96744 Kaneohe, Honolulu,
Hawaii, USA

BORN: 10 Nov 1904

Died: Jul 1985

State (Year) SSN
Issued: Hawaii (Before 1951)

SAVE   Cancel

Write a comment

Make a Connection

Find others who are researching
William Kamaka in Public Member
Trees

Source Citation
Number: 575-05-6395; Issue State: Hawaii; Issue Date: Before 1951

Source Information
Ancestry.com. U.S., Social Security Death Index, 1935-2014 [database on-line]. Provo, UT,
USA: Ancestry.com Operations Inc., 2011.

Original data: Social Security Administration. Social Security Death Index, Master File.
Social Security Administration.

Description
The Social Security Administration Death Master File contains information on millions
of deceased individuals with United States social security numbers whose deaths were
reported to the Social Security Administration. Birth years for the individuals listed
range from 1875 to last year. Information in these records includes name, birth date,
death date, and last known residence. Learn more

ancestry

All results for Joseph Kamaka

Search Filters
Joseph
Kamaka
BORN 1906
Waikane, Ho...

COLLECTION All Collections

Edit Search   New Search

Results 1–20 of 17,167

RECORDS   CATEGORIES

Matching Person (from family trees)

See more like this ...

Birth: 23 Dec 1906
Death: Jul 1978 - Kaneohe, Honolulu,
Hawaii, United States of America
Parents: John Kaoholowahi
Kamaka, Annie Kahonuanuioka'u Hatton

Joseph K Kamaka
KAMAKA FAMILY TREE

All Categories

> Census & Voter Lists
> Birth, Marriage & Death
> Military
> Immigration & Travel
Newspapers &
Publications
Pictures
> Stories, Memories &
Histories
Maps, Atlases &
Gazetteers
> Schools, Directories &
Church Histories
> Wills, Probates, Land,
Tax & Criminal
> Reference, Dictionaries
& Almanacs
Family Trees

Shortcut Keys ▸

Matching Records

1940 United States Federal Census
CENSUS & VOTER LISTS

View Image

NAME **Joseph Kamaka**
BIRTH abt 1906 - Hawaii
RESIDENCE 1935
RESIDENCE Koolaupoko, Honolulu,
Hawaii

1930 United States Federal Census
CENSUS & VOTER LISTS

View Image

NAME **Joseph K Kamaka**
BIRTH abt 1907 - Hawaii
RESIDENCE 1930 - Koolaupoko,
Honolulu, Hawaii Territory

U.S., Social Security Death Index,
1935-2014
BIRTH, MARRIAGE & DEATH

NAME **Joseph Kamaka**
BIRTH 23 Dec 1906
DEATH Jul 1978 - Kaneohe,
Honolulu, Hawaii, USA
GIRL Hawaii

1920 United States Federal Census
CENSUS & VOTER LISTS

View Image

NAME **Joseph Kamaka**
BIRTH abt 1902 - Hawaii
RESIDENCE 1920 - Honolulu, Honolulu,
Hawaii Territory

1910 United States Federal Census
CENSUS & VOTER LISTS

View Image

NAME **Joseph Kamaka**
BIRTH abt 1910 - Hawaii
RESIDENCE 1910 - Wailuku, Maui, Hawaii
Territory

NAME Samuel Joseph Kamaka

ancestry

All Public Member Trees results for Joseph Kamaka

Results 1-1 of 1

Member Tree	Name	Parents
KAMAKA Family Tree	Joseph K Kamaka	F: John Kaoholowahi Kamaka
Public Member Tree 1 source	Birth: 23 Dec 1906 Death: Jul 1978 - Kaneohe, Honolulu, Hawaii, United States of America	M: Annie Kahonuanuioka'u Hatton

1-1 of 1

Per page   20

ancestry

Joseph K Kamaka
in the 1930 United States Federal Census

Name:	Joseph K Kamaka
Birth Year:	abt 1907
Gender:	Male
Race:	Hawaiian
Birthplace:	Hawaii
Marital Status:	Single
Relation to Head of House:	Son
Home in 1930:	Koolaupoko, Honolulu, Hawaii Territory
Map of Home:	View Map
Able to Read and Write:	No
Father's Birthplace:	Hawaii
Mother's Birthplace:	Hawaii

Household Members:

Name	Age
John Kamaka	52
Annie Kamaka	50
John K Kamaka	30
Charles M Kamaka	29
Henrietta Kamaka	27
William K Kamaka	25
Joseph K Kamaka	23
Ronald L Kamaka	21
Thelma K Kamaka	18
Lucy K Kamaka	16
Rachel H Kamaka	13
Abraham K Kamaka	9
Alfred K Morita	23
Annie K Morita	20
Alfred K Morita	2
John K Kuahilo	35
Daniel P Kaialau	35

Source Citation

Year: 1930; Census Place: Koolaupoko, Honolulu, Hawaii Territory; Roll: 2626; Page: 2D; Enumeration District: 0123; Image: 115.0; FHL microfilm: 2342916

Source Information

Ancestry.com. 1930 United States Federal Census [database on-line]. Provo, UT, USA: Ancestry.com Operations Inc, 2002.

Original data: United States of America, Bureau of the Census. Fifteenth Census of the United States, 1930. Washington, D.C.: National Archives and Records Administration, 1930. T626, 2,667 rolls.

Joseph K Kamaka

BIRTH 23 DEC 1906 • Hawaiian Islands

DEATH JUL 1978 • Kaneohe, Honolulu, Hawaii, United States of America

Facts

Age 0 — Birth
23 Dec 1906 • Hawaiian Islands

Age 1 — Birth of Brother John Kamakananahukilani Kamaka (1908–1980)
1908 • Koolaupoko, Honolulu, Hawaii Territory

Age 1 — Birth of Brother Ronald Kamakananahukilani Kamaka (1908–1980)
6 April 1908 • Honolulu, Honolulu, Hawaii, USA

Age 1 — Birth of Half-Brother John Kamakananahukilani Kamaka (1908–1980)
6 Apr 1908 • Honolulu HI

Age 2 — Death of Half-Sister Rachel N Kamaka (–1908)
1908 • Hawaii

Age 4 — Birth of Sister Annie K Kamaka (1910–1993)
abt 1910 • Honolulu HI

Age 5 — Birth of Half-Sister Thelma K Kamaka (1912–1963)
abt 1912 • Hawaii

Age 5 — Birth of Half-Sister Thelma K Kamaka (1912–1963)
1912 • Hawaii, USA

Age 5 — Birth of Half-Sister Lucy Kapaeloa Kamaka (1912–2001)
3 Mar 1912 • Koolaupoko, Honolulu, Hawaii Territory

Age 29 — Death of Father John Kaoholowahi Kamaka (1877–1936)
6 Jan 1936 • Honolulu, Hawaii, United States

Age 46 — Death of Mother Annie Kahonuanuioka'u Hatton (1880–1952)
27 Dec 1952 • Honolulu, Hawaii, United States

Age 57 — Death of Half-Sister Thelma K Kamaka (1912–1963)
1963

Age 57 — Death of Half-Sister Thelma K Kamaka (1912–1963)
1963

Age 61 — Death of Brother Charles M Kamaka (1900–1968)
17 Jan 1968 • Honolulu HI

Age 61 — Death of Half-Brother Charles M Kamaka (1900–1968)
17 Jan 1968 • Honolulu HI

Age 71 — Death
Jul 1978 • Kaneohe, Honolulu, Hawaii, United States of America

Sources

Ancestry Sources

Ancestry Family Trees

Family

Parents

John Kaoholowahi Kamaka 1877–1936

Annie Kahonuanuioka'u Hatton 1880–1952

Spouse

ancestry

Ronald K Kamaka
in the 1940 United States Federal Census

📄 View blank form

✏️ Add alternate information

⚠️ Report issue

Name:	Ronald K Kamaka
Age:	32
Estimated birth year:	abt 1908
Gender:	Male
Race:	Part Hawaiian (Hawaiian)
Birthplace:	Hawaii
Marital Status:	Married
Relation to Head of House:	Brother
Home in 1940:	Honolulu, Honolulu, Hawaii
Map of Home in 1940:	View Map
Street:	N Kuakini Street
House Number:	421
Sheet Number:	2B
Occupation:	Truck Driver
Attended School or College:	No
Highest Grade Completed:	Elementary school, 4th grade
Hours Worked Week Prior to Census:	16
Class of Worker:	Wage or salary worker
Weeks Worked in 1939:	40
Income:	1300
Income Other Sources:	No
Neighbors:	View others on page

Household Members:

Name	Age
John K Kamaka	40
Annie K Morita	29
Ronald K Kamaka	32

Provided in association with National Archives and Records Administration

Suggested Records ❓

📄 1920 United States Federal Census
Kalani Kamaka

📄 1930 United States Federal Census
Ronald L Kamaka

📄 U.S., Social Security Death Index, 1935-2014
Ronald Kamaka

📄 U.S. City Directories, 1822-1995
Ronald K Kamaka

📄 www.BillionGraves.com Burial Index
Ronald K Kamaka

Write a comment

Make a Connection

Find others who are researching Ronald K Kamaka in Public Member Trees

Name	Age
Polly Kamaka	19
McRonald Kamaka	3
Raymond Kamaka	11/12
Robert L Cooper	30
Lucy Cooper	26
Betty Lou Cooper	3
Robert Cooper	1
Miguel Kelihupakako	21
Rachel Kelihupakako	23
Aileen Kelihupakako	9/12

SAVE Cancel

Source Citation

Year: 1940; Census Place: Honolulu, Honolulu, Hawaii; Roll: T627_4588; Page: 2B; Enumeration District: 2-166

Source Information

Ancestry.com. 1940 United States Federal Census [database on-line]. Provo, UT, USA: Ancestry.com Operations, Inc., 2012.

Original data: United States of America, Bureau of the Census. Sixteenth Census of the United States, 1940. Washington, D.C.: National Archives and Records Administration, 1940. T627, 4,643 rolls.

Description

The 1940 United States Federal Census is the largest census released to date and the most recent census available for public access. The census gives us a glimpse into the lives of Americans in 1940, with details about a household's occupants that include birthplaces, occupations, education, citizenship, and income. Learn more...

ancestry

All results for Ronald Kamaka

Search FiltersFilters Exact

Ronald

Kamaka

born 1907

and Waikane, Ho...

COLLECTION   All Collections

Edit Search   New Search

All Categories

  Pictures

  Family Trees

Shortcut Keys ▸

Results 1-1 of 1

Matching Person (from family trees)

Ronald Kamakananahukilani Kamaka
Carolyn's Greys family tree

Birth: 6 Apr 1908 - Honolulu

Death: 07 Dec 1980 (7 Dec 1980) -
Kaneohe, Honolulu, Hawaii, United
States of America

Parents: John Kaoholowahi
Kamaka, Ane Kahonuanuioka'u Aalona
Hatton

Matching Records

Private Member Photos

PICTURES

1-1 of 1

RECORDS   CATEGORIES

See more like this ...

PHOTO: Ronald
Kamakananahukilani
Kamaka-pic
CAPTION: Portrait
TAKEN: Unknown - Unknown
ATTACHED TO: Ronald
Kamakananahukilani
Kamaka (born 1908)

Per page   20

ancestry

All Family Trees results for Ronald Kamaka

Search Filters Filters

Ronald

Kamaka

BORN 1907

ANY Waikane, Ho...

COLLECTION   All Collections

Edit Search   New Search

All Categories

Family Trees

Private Member Trees

Public Member Trees

Shortcut Keys ▸

Results 1–6 of 6

Catryna Griep family tree
PUBLIC MEMBER TREE

2 attached records, 3 sources

RECORDS   CATEGORIES

Ronald
NAME Kamakananahukilani
Kamaka
BIRTH 6 Apr 1908 - Honolulu
07 Dec 1980 (7 Dec 1980) -
DEATH Kaneohe, Honolulu, Hawaii,
United States of America
John Kaoholowahi
Kamaka, Ane
PARENTS Kahonuanuioka'u Aalona
Hatton

The author of this tree asked us to keep it private. Ask them nicely and they might share.

Kamaka Ohana

Personal Member Tree

4 attached records, 5 sources

Ek photos NAME **Ronald Kamakananahukilani**
Kamaka
BIRTH 1908 - Honolulu

The author of this tree asked us to keep it private. Ask them nicely and they might share.

Trenkle - Forney

Personal Member Tree

8 attached records, 9 sources

Ek photos NAME **Ronald Kamakananahukilani**
Kamaka
BIRTH 1908 - Honolulu

The author of this tree asked us to keep it private. Ask them nicely and they might share.

Anisa Butler family tree

Personal Member Tree

2 attached records, 3 sources

Ek photos NAME **Ronald Kamakananahukilani**
Kamaka
BIRTH 1908 - Honolulu

Posted on: Sunday, August 19, 2007

A villain fans loved to hate

By Lee Cataluna
Advertiser Columnist

He was a man known by many names. He traveled the world and held jobs as widely different as bouncer and doughnut maker. And somehow, though he played a bad guy, people loved him more than the good guys.

McRonald Keli Kamaka, 71, passed away on July 23 in Saskatoon, Saskatchewan, Canada. Here in Hawai'i, we knew him as Tor Kamaka, villain suprema on 50th State Wrestling with Lord Blears and Ed Francis in the 1970s. Some listings show his ring names as Mr. Moto, Dr. Moto, Killer Moto and Killer Tor Kamaka. But in Canada, where wrestling is an even bigger draw than it was back here, fans came to know him as Tor Kamata,

McRonald Keli
Kamaka

with a "T" at the end, a name he gave himself while he was wrestling in Japan.

"It's the story of a country boy who went away and did good for himself," says cousin Judy Tsutsui, who grew up with Kamaka on the family's land in Waikane, where Kamaka was raised by his grandparents. After graduating from Castle High School in 1956, Kamaka served in the Air Force and was stationed in Turkey. When he came home, he worked as a bouncer at Queen's Surf and came under the tutelage of wrestling notables Lord Blears, Neph Maiava, Curtis Iaukea and Tosh Togo.

In the late 1970s in Hawai'i, professional wrestling was more than sport, more than entertainment — it was a phenomenon. Crowds packed the Blaisdell Arena and families wired up together on Friday Nights to watch Big Time Wrestling matches on KGMB-TV. Little boys wanted to be just like their favorite wrestlers. They practiced moves like the Atomic Drop on the playground equipment. Tor Kamaka, 5-feet-10 and 350 pounds, evil sneer and dirty tricks, was the bad guy you cheered for. When he showed up, things were bound to get interesting.

He'd throw salt in the good guys' eyes. He'd pull a chain or some other sort of devised weaponry out of his trunks. He'd eat a goldfish during a television interview. The crowds loved it, but his grandparents weren't sure what to think.

"His grandma and grandpa, we used to take them to go and watch and they used to ask him, 'But why do you have to be the bad guy?'" Tsutsui recalls. "And he would say, 'Because, Grandma, that makes more money. I have a family to support.'"

Tsutsui says Kamaka told stories about traveling from state to state and having to park the car away from the arena and take a cab inside so as not to be noticed by fans who loved to hate him. Some people, women included, got so worked up, they threw their shoes at him. "He worked so hard to have people hate him," his cousin says with a laugh.

Kamaka lived in Kansas for a time, where his two eldest children were born. Later, he brought them home to Hawai'i. When he remarried, he moved to Canada with his wife. He had six children.

In Canada, Tor Kamata, as he was called, was a star of the Stampede Wrestling circuit, beloved and quoted by children. StarPhoenix columnist John Gormley wrote, Kamata "would promise the ring announcer Ed Whalen exotic gifts and silks from Japan and the Orient. But being a heel, Kamata would weasel out of his promises with the memorable words 'No chancee, Mis-tah Whalen.' This became his trademark. And, for a time, everyone from kids to teachers and even parents would often prefer the 'no chancee' retort to just saying no."

Kamaka won many wrestling titles during his career, including tag team belts in the U.S. and Japan. He was the first non-Japanese to hold a title belt in that country. He is in the Wrestling Hall of Fame both in Canada and the U.S.

In a sport that mixes theater with athleticism, Kamaka excelled at both.

"There is a picture that we have of him. He was a big person. He was huge. We have a picture of him that shows him jumping up above the rope. He was wrestling this person from Japan, Giant Baba, and he knocked him out with a kick," Tsutsui recalls with admiration in her voice. "If he didn't bring that picture home, we wouldn't have believed him."

After retiring from the sport, Kamaka came home to Hawai'i and, for a time, ran a doughnut wagon.

"It was small doughnuts, good doughnuts, and shave ice. He started here in Waikane in the front yard and then they went to Wai'anae down the beach side."

His obituary in Canada's StarPhoenix also says he ran a restaurant and practiced shiatsu.

And in his retirement, he enjoyed his children and six grandchildren. "He was really just a jelly-belly, you know. He really was a softie, a very kind person," Tsutsui says.

Daughter-in-law Joelvonne Kamaka of Wailuku called him a teddy bear and a loving family man, who came to Hawai'i often to see his grandkids, welcomed their visits in Canada and often met Hawai'i relatives "halfway" in Vegas, where he was constantly recognized by Hawai'i people who remembered his wrestling career. "Lots of people remember him, even more than the good guys," she says.

A memorial and prayer service will be held for Kamaka today at 11 a.m. at the family's land, 48-437 Kamehameha Highway in Waikane with scattering of ashes to follow. Tsutsui says, "He traveled quite a bit, and now he's coming home. That's what he wanted."

Leo Cataluna's column runs Tuesdays, Fridays and Sundays. Reach her at 535-8172 or lcataluna@honoluluadvertiser.com

ESCORTED TOURS OF JAPAN

Adventures in Discovering Traditional Japan

Carol and Ruth; son, Harry Jr.; sisters, Kiyome Matsukawa, Shizume Izumi and Fujie Shishido. Private service held. Arrangements by Dodo Mortuary, Kona.

TOMMY TSUTOMU KAKESAKO, 85, of Honolulu, died Aug. 3, 2007. Born in Papa'ikou, South Hilo, Hawai'i. Co-owner of Kakesako Brothers; certified gemologist /watchmaker; member of the 442nd Regimental Combat Team, Company L. Survived by brother, Michael; sister, Joyce Toshie Inao. Visitation 3 to 4 p.m. Sunday at Hosoi Garden Mortuary; service 4 p.m. No flowers. Casual attire.

McRONALD "TOR" KELII KAMAKA, 71, of Saskatoon, Saskatchewan, died July 23, 2007. Born on O'ahu. A professional wrestler; first non-Japanese title belt-holder and tag team champion in Japan; member of Canada and U.S. Wrestling halls of fame. Survived by brothers, Stanley, Raymond, Albert, Benjamin, Charles and Daniel; sisters, Yvonne and Helene; children, Leilani Zabart, Curtis, Kalani, Ryan, Alaina and Sharlene; six grandchildren. Service 11 a.m. Sunday at 48-437 Kamehameha Highway, Waikane; scattering of ashes to follow. Casual attire. Arrangements by Martens Warmen Funeral Home, Warman, SK S0K 4S0, Canada.

ALBERT KATSUMI KURIKI, 74, of Lihu'e, Kaua'i, died Aug. 4, 2007. Born in Lihu'e. Survived by wife, Jane; sons, Byron, Clayton and Curtis; daughters, Colleen Okada and Laura Kuriki; 11 grandchildren; one great-grandchild; sisters, Rita Nakashige, June Iha and Kate Setoda. Private service held. Donations to Hospice Kauai. Arrangements by Garden Island Mortuary.

AUDREY LEE KWOCK, 69, of Honolulu, died Aug. 6, 2007. Born in Honolulu. Survived by son, Douglas; daughters, Lori Tolentino and Karin Martin; brothers, Donald and Wilfred Lee; sisters, Ethel Tan, Beatrice Wing and Helen Lum; eight grandchildren. Visitation 3 to 4 p.m. Sunday at Nuuanu Memorial Park & Mortuary; service 4 p.m. Aloha attire.

RODNEY "HOTROD" VIDAL LOPEZ, 57, of Kailua, Kona, Hawaii, died Aug. 5, 2007. Born in Pahala, Hawai'i. Painter for the former Kona Surf Hotel. Survived by wife, Kanani; daughters, Ulu McKeipin, Kanani, Valerie, and Leesa; brothers, Roy, Decky, Cyril and Daryl; sisters, June Nerito, Sandi Ramos and Tacy Lopez; 17 grandchildren. Visitation 9 to 10 a.m. Saturday at the Big Island Game Fishing Clubhouse, Honokohau Harbor, Kailua, Kona; service 10 a.m. Casual attire. Arrangements by Dodo Mortuary, Kona.

EUFEMIA CORPUZ MACABEO, 84, of Kahului, Maui, died Aug. 5, 2007. Born in Narvacan, Ilocos Sur, Philippines. Housekeeper at the Napili Shores Resort. Survived by sons, Elmer and Perfecto; daughters, Francisca Julian, Visitacion De Castro and Paz Colcol; sisters, Florencia Raquel and Pilarina Cabitac; 14 grandchildren; six great-grandchildren. Visitation 6 p.m. Friday at the Kahului Full Gospel Temple; service 7 to 8 p.m. Visitation also 8:45 a.m. Saturday at the church; service 9 a.m.; burial 10:30 a.m. at Maui Memorial Park. Casual attire. Arrangements by Nakamura Mortuary.

NORMAN KAPIINAOKALANI MAKALENA SR., 76, of Honolulu, died Aug. 2, 2007. Born in Honolulu. Survived by sons, Norman Jr. and Warren; daughters, Wendy Volivar, Sandra and Suzanne; brother, Daniel; sister, Marilyn; three grandchildren. Visitation 10:30 a.m. to noon Monday at Diamond Head Mortuary; service noon; burial to follow at Diamond Head Memorial Park. Casual attire.

CARMEN "PATTI GIRL" KAMELA NAEHU, 64, of Honolulu, died Aug. 9, 2007. Born in Honolulu. Retired from Dole Cannery and the Halekoa Hotel. Survived by mother, Wilhelmina; brothers, Gordon, Samuel, Cedric and Clayton; sisters, Gwendolyn Kaleikini, Ruth, Holly and Wilhelmina; companion, Sandy. Visitation 5 to 9 p.m. Friday at Mililani Downtown Mortuary; service 6 p.m.; cremation to follow. Aloha attire.

RAY NOBORU OTANI, 60, of Kea'au, Hawai'i, died Aug. 5, 2007. Born in Hilo, Hawai'i. An estimator for the former Fair Contracting. Survived by daughters, Raylynn Carvalho and Renee; sisters, Mildred DeMattos and Darlene Martin; three grandchildren. Graveside urn service 11 a.m. Saturday at Hawaii Veterans Cemetery No. 2. Please bring a written story you would like to share about him for a family album. Casual attire. Arrangements by Dodo Mortuary, Hilo.

JONNETTE "NOE" HENDERSON ROQUE, 42, of Wai'anae, died Aug. 6, 2007. Born in Honolulu. Maile Elementary School teacher's aide. Survived by husband, Anthony; sons, Mikey, Nicholas, Tyler and Anthony Jr.; parents, Rannie "Bulla" and Stephanie Henderson; brother, Rannie Henderson Jr.; sisters, Elizabeth "Lisa" Thcomb, Nicole Henderson and Brandy De Ramos; caregiver, Uesa Potoae. Visitation 5 p.m. Thursday at Mililani Mortuary Makai Chapel; service 6:30 p.m. Flowers welcome. Casual attire. Arrangements by Mililani Mortuary.

JULIAN ULEP ULEP, 80, of Honolulu, died July 26, 2007. Born in the Philippines. Retired Hawaiian Dredging laborer. Survived by wife, Mary; daughters, Blandina Leonin, Perpetua Barba and Magdalena Doctolero; hanai daughter, Filomina Pasion; sons, Romualdo, Jose Rizal Ulep; 18

ancestry

Polly Kamaka

in the 1940 United States Federal Census

View blank form

Add alternate information

Report issue

Name:	Polly Kamaka
Age:	19
Estimated birth year:	abt 1921
Gender:	Female
Race:	Part-Hawaiian (Hawaiian)
Birthplace:	Hawaii
Marital Status:	Married
Relation to Head of House:	Sister-in-law
Home in 1940:	Honolulu, Honolulu, Hawaii
Map of Home in 1940:	View Map
Street:	N Kuakini Street
House Number:	421
Sheet Number:	2B
Attended School or College:	No
Highest Grade Completed:	Elementary school, 8th grade
Weeks Worked in 1939:	0
Income:	0
Income Other Sources:	No
Neighbors:	View others on page

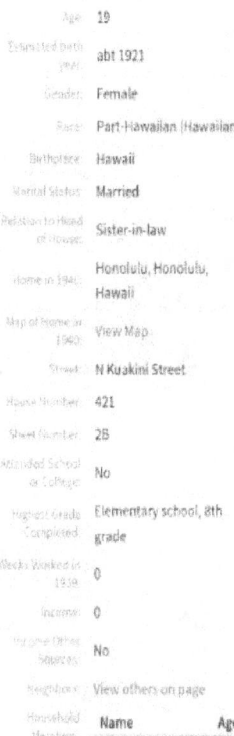

Household Members:	Name	Age
	John K Kamaka	40
	Annie K Morita	29
	Ronald K Kamaka	32
	Polly Kamaka	19
	McRonald Kamaka	3

11/12

Provided in association with National Archives and Records Administration

Suggested Records

1940 United States Federal Census
Mary P Kamaka

Write a comment.

Make a Connection

Find others who are researching Polly Kamaka in Public Member Trees

ancestry

All results for Thelma Kamaka Chung

ancestry

Thelma K Kamaka
in the 1930 United States Federal Census

View blank form

Add alternate information

Report issue

Name:	Thelma K Kamaka
Birth Year:	abt 1912
Gender:	Female
Race:	Hawaiian
Birthplace:	Hawaii
Marital Status:	Single
Relation to Head of House:	Daughter
Home in 1930:	Koolaupoko, Honolulu, Hawaii Territory
Map of Home:	View Map
Able to Read and Write:	No
Father's Birthplace:	Hawaii
Mother's Birthplace:	Hawaii

Household Members:

Name	Age
John Kamaka	52
Annie Kamaka	50
John K Kamaka	30
Charles M Kamaka	29
Henrietta Kamaka	27
William K Kamaka	25
Joseph K Kamaka	23
Ronald L Kamaka	21
Thelma K Kamaka	18
Lucy K Kamaka	16
Rachel H Kamaka	13

Provided in association with National Archives and Records Administration

Suggested Records

1940 United States Federal Census
Kapua Kamaka

Write a comment.

Make a Connection

Find others who are researching Thelma K Kamaka in Public Member Trees

COOPER, LUCY KAPAELOA

Age 60, of 4847 I-C Kani Hwy, Kaneohe, passed away April 8, at Kaneohe Hospital. Born in Waialua. Sept 26, 1913. She was a member of Koolaupoko Hawaiian Civic Club and Kaneohe Senior Citizens. Survived by husband Robert Lewis Cooper; daughters, Mrs. Betty Lou Ahki, Mrs. Ralph Hada Maae Tualaulelei, Mrs. David (Jeanne Lehei Carnel; sons, Robert Jr. (Elizabeth), Daniel Kalani Iwaika (deceased), David (Katherine) & William Cooper; 15 grandchildren, 3 sisters, Henrietta Pahoa, Anne Kalilah & Rachel Lee; 4 brothers, William, Ronald, Joe & Abraham Kamaka.

FRIENDS MAY CALL FROM 6-9 P.M. WEDNESDAY, APRIL 10 AT HAWAIIAN MEMORIAL PARK MORTUARY. SERVICES 8 P.M. AND AGAIN ON THURS., APRIL 11th FROM 9-11 A.M. SERVICES 11 A.M. BURIAL TO FOLLOW IN HAWAIIAN MEMORIAL PARK CEMETERY. ARRANGEMENTS BY HAWAIIAN MEMORIAL PARK MORTUARY.

ancestry

Rachel Nainoa Uu

in the U.S., Social Security Applications and Claims Index, 1936-2007

No Image
Text only collection

🖊 Add alternate information

⚠ Report issue

Name	Rachel Nainoa Uu [Rachel N Uu] [Rachel Nainoa Kamaka]
SSN	576368774
Gender	Female
Birth Date	10 Jan 1917
Birth Place	Waikane Kool, Hawaii
Death Date	29 May 1992
Father	John K Kamaka
Mother	Annie E Hatton
Type of Claim	Original SSN
Notes	Jul 1956: Name listed as RACHEL NAINOA UU; 25 Jul 1992: Name listed as RACHEL N UU

SAVE ⌄   Cancel

Suggested Records ❓

🗋 1930 United States Federal Census
Rachel H Kamaka

🗋 U.S., Social Security Death Index, 1935-2014
Rachel Uu

🗋 1930 United States Federal Census
Rachel Kamaka

🗋 1940 United States Federal Census
Rachael Kamaka

Write a comment

Make a Connection

Find others who are researching Rachel Nainoa Uu in Public Member Trees

Source Information
Ancestry.com. *U.S., Social Security Applications and Claims Index, 1936-2007* [database on-line]. Provo, UT, USA: Ancestry.com Operations, Inc., 2015.

Original data: Social Security Applications and Claims, 1936-2007.

Description
This database picks up where the SSDI leaves off, with details such as birth date and parents' names extracted from information filed with the Social Security Administration through the application or claims process. Learn more...

Star ★ Advertiser

HONOLULU STAR-ADVERTISER OBITUARIES

» MARY JOSEITA NISHIDA
Peter "Bingo" Waiola Kalae Kaohookapua »

Daniel Kealoha Kamaka

Posted On December 30th, 2016 - Honolulu Star-Advertiser Obituaries

Share

66, of Kaneohe, Hawaii, died in Waikane on Sunday, December 11, 2016. He was born in Honolulu. Services: 10:30am on Thursday, January 12 at 46-477 Kamehameha Highway, Kamaka Place (Al's house). Scattering of ashes to follow. Posted in Death Notices

Denotes U.S. Military Veteran

· Search Hawaii Obituaries

· View Obituaries By Day

· Obituaries Category
  • Death Notices
  • Family Placed Obituaries
  • Featured

· Hawaii Obituaries
  • Obituaries RSS

· How to place an Obituary

ancestry

Abraham K Kamaka
in the U.S., World War II Army Enlistment Records, 1938-1946

No Image
First only collection

Add alternate information

Report Issue

Name:	Abraham K Kamaka
Birth Year:	1921
Race:	Others, citizen
Nativity State or Country:	Hawaii
State of Residence:	Hawaii
Enlistment Date:	1 Aug 1944
Branch:	No branch assignment
Branch Code:	No branch assignment
Grade:	Private
Grade Code:	Private
Term of Enlistment:	Enlistment for the duration of the War or other emergency, plus six months, subject to the discretion of the President or otherwise according to law
Component:	Selectees (Enlisted Men)
Source:	Civil Life
Education:	Grammar school
Civil Occupation:	Semiskilled chauffeurs and drivers, bus, taxi, truck, and tractor
Marital Status:	Single, without dependents
Height:	00
Weight:	000

Provided in association with
National Archives and Records
Administration

Suggested Records

1930 United States Federal Census
Abraham K Kamaka

Write a comment

Make a Connection

Find others who are researching
Abraham K Kamaka in Public
Member Trees

SAVE ∨   Cancel

CERTIFICATION OF VITAL RECORD

TYPE OR PRINT IN PERMANENT BLACK INK

241RG

ID TAG NO. 116612

Local File Number 265

OREGON DEPARTMENT OF HUMAN RESOURCES
HEALTH DIVISION
CENTER FOR HEALTH STATISTICS 136
CERTIFICATE OF DEATH

State File Number

DECEDENT

DECEDENT'S NAME: First — Betty | Middle — Lou K | Last — ARMSTRONG | SEX — female | DATE OF DEATH (Month, Day, Year) — May 14, 1992

SOCIAL SECURITY NUMBER — 575 34 5225 | AGE Last Birthday (Years) — 55 | Under 1 Year | Under 1 Day | BIRTHPLACE (City and State or Foreign Country) — Honolulu, Hawaii | DATE OF BIRTH (Month, Day, Year) — July 1, 1936

WAS DECEDENT EVER IN U.S. ARMED FORCES? ☐ Yes ☒ No

FACILITY NAME (If not institution, give street and number) — 14583 N. Bluegrass Lane

PLACE OF DEATH: ☒ Decedent's Home

CITY, TOWN, OR LOCATION OF DEATH — Sisters | COUNTY OF DEATH — Deschutes

DECEDENT'S USUAL OCCUPATION — Factory Operator | KIND OF BUSINESS/INDUSTRY — Wool & Garment | MARITAL STATUS — Married | SPOUSE (If married, widowed) — Thomas

RESIDENCE STATE — Oregon | COUNTY — Deschutes | CITY, TOWN OR LOCATION — Sisters | STREET AND NUMBER — 14583 N. Bluegrass Lane

INSIDE CITY LIMITS? ☐ Yes ☐ No | ZIP CODE — 97759 | RACE — White | DECEDENT'S EDUCATION — Secondary 12

PARENTS

FATHER NAME: First — Robert | Middle | Last — Cooper | MOTHER NAME: First — Lucy | Middle | Last — Kanaka

INFORMANT — NAME and relationship to Deceased — Thomas Armstrong, husband

DISPOSITION

METHOD OF DISPOSITION | PLACE OF DISPOSITION — Hawaiian Memorial Park | LOCATION City or Town, State — Kaneohe, Hawaii

SIGNATURE OF FUNERAL SERVICE LICENSEE — (signature) | LICENSE NUMBER — 3331 | NAME, ADDRESS AND ZIP OF FACILITY — Niswonger-Reynolds, Inc 105 N.W. Irving Bend, Oregon 97701

REGISTRAR

DATE FILED (Month, Day, Year) — May 18, 1992 | REGISTRAR'S SIGNATURE — Jacqueline Mathis Dep

CERTIFIER

TIME OF DEATH — 2:55 P. | WAS MEDICAL EXAMINER NOTIFIED? ☐ Yes ☒ No

To the best of my knowledge, death occurred at the time, date, place and due to the cause(s) and manner stated. (Signature)

DATE SIGNED (Month, Day, Year) — May 14, 1992

NAME, TITLE, ADDRESS AND ZIP OF CERTIFIER — Stephen B. Kornfeld, M.D., 1501 N.E. Medical Center Dr., Bend, OR 97701

CAUSE OF DEATH

PART I — IMMEDIATE CAUSE (a) — Breast Cancer

MANNER OF DEATH — ☒ Natural

THIS IS A TRUE AND EXACT REPRODUCTION OF THE DOCUMENT OFFICIALLY REGISTERED AT THE OFFICE OF THE DESCHUTES COUNTY REGISTRAR.

DATE ISSUED — May 18, 1992

FLORENCE ABEND-TORRIGINO
COUNTY REGISTRAR
DESCHUTES COUNTY, OREGON

ancestry

Children (0)

Robert Lewis Cooper Jr

B: August 11, 1938 in Honolulu, Honolulu, Hawaii, USA
D: October 2006 in Honolulu County, Hawaii, USA

Parents
Robert Lewis Cooper
1911-1978

Lucy Kapaeloa Kamaka
1913-1974

Robert Lewis Kawailiul Cooper Sr.
in the U.S., Social Security Death Index, 1935-2014

No Image
Text only collection

Name	Robert Lewis Kawailiul Cooper Sr.
Last Residence	96816 Honolulu, Honolulu, Hawaii
BORN	11 Aug 1938
Died	13 Oct 2007
State (Year) SSN issued	Hawaii (1952)

Request copy of original application

Add alternate information

Report issue

SAVE ∨   Cancel

Write a comment

Make a Connection

Find others who are researching Robert Lewis Kawailiul Cooper Sr. in Public Member Trees

Source Citation
Issue State: *Hawaii*, Issue Date: *1952*

Source Information
Ancestry.com. U.S., *Social Security Death Index, 1935-2014* [database on-line]. Provo, UT, USA: Ancestry.com Operations Inc, 2011.

Original data: Social Security Administration. *Social Security Death Index, Master File.* Social Security Administration.

Description
The Social Security Administration Death Master File contains information on millions of deceased individuals with United States social security numbers whose deaths were reported to the Social Security Administration. Birth years for the individuals listed range from 1875 to last year. Information in these records includes name, birth date, death date, and last known residence. Learn more...

ancestry

Children (0)

Robert Lewis Cooper Jr

B: August 11, 1936 in Honolulu, Honolulu, Hawaii, USA
D: October 2008 in Honolulu County, Hawaii, USA

Parents
Robert Lewis Cooper
1911-1976

Lucy Kapaeloa Kamaka
1913-1974

All results for Robert Lewis Cooper

Robert Lewis
Cooper
BORN 1936
Honolulu,...
DEATH 2006
Honolulu C...
MORE SEARCHES OR Show All ⌄

COLLECTION All Collections

Edit Search New Search

All Categories

> Census & Voter Lists
> Birth, Marriage & Death
> Military
> Immigration & Travel
> Newspapers & Publications
Pictures
> Stories, Memories & Histories
Maps, Atlases & Gazetteers
> Schools, Directories & Church Histories
> Wills, Probates, Land, Tax & Criminal

Results 1–20 of 462,003

U.S., Social Security Death Index, 1935-2014
BIRTH, MARRIAGE & DEATH

1940 United States Federal Census
CENSUS & VOTER LISTS
View Image

1940 United States Federal Census
CENSUS & VOTER LISTS
View Image

1940 United States Federal Census
CENSUS & VOTER LISTS
View Image

U.S., School Yearbooks, 1880-2012
SCHOOLS, DIRECTORIES & CHURCH HISTORIES
View Image

U.S., School Yearbooks, 1880-2012
SCHOOLS, DIRECTORIES & CHURCH HISTORIES
View Image

RECORDS CATEGORIES

NAME **Robert Lewis Kawailiul Cooper** Sr.
BIRTH 11 Aug 1938
DEATH 13 Oct 2007 - Honolulu, Honolulu, Hawaii
CIVIL Hawaii

NAME **Robert E Cooper**
OTHER Joan L
BIRTH abt 1931 - Oregon
RESIDENCE 1935
RESIDENCE Honolulu, Honolulu, Hawaii

NAME **Robert Cooper 2nd**
BIRTH abt 1939 - Hawaii
RESIDENCE Honolulu, Honolulu, Hawaii

NAME **Robert Cooper**
BIRTH abt 1932 - Philippine Islands
RESIDENCE 1935
RESIDENCE Honolulu, Honolulu, Hawaii

NAME **Robert Cooper**
BIRTH abt 1933
RESIDENCE 1949 - Honolulu, Hawaii, USA

NAME **Robert Cooper**
BIRTH abt 1933
RESIDENCE 1949 - Honolulu, Hawaii, USA

ancestry

All results for Judy Mae Cooper Tsutsui

Results 1–20 of 313 | RECORDS CATEGORIES

U.S., Social Security Death Index,
1935-2014 — Judy Mae Puahaunani Tsutsui
BIRTH 15 Mar 1943
DEATH 2 Dec 2009 - Kaneohe, Honolulu, Hawaii
Hawaii

U.S. Public Records Index, 1950-1993, Volume 1 — Judy M Tsutsui
BIRTH 1 Nov 1943
RESIDENCE 1992 - Kaneohe, HI

U.S. Public Records Index, 1950-1993, Volume 1 — Judy Mp Tsutsui
BIRTH 1 Nov 1943
RESIDENCE 1993 - Kaneohe, HI [Kaneohe, HI]

U.S. Public Records Index, 1950-1993, Volume 1 — Phyllis M Tsutsui
BIRTH 1 Jan 1946
RESIDENCE 1988 - Waimanalo, HI [Waipahu, HI]

U.S. Public Records Index, 1950-1993, Volume 1 — Shirley M Tsutsui
BIRTH 15 Nov 1946
RESIDENCE 1992 - Waipahu, HI

U.S. Public Records Index, 1950-1993, Volume 1 — Melvin M Tsutsui
BIRTH 1 Sep 1948
RESIDENCE 1993 - Honolulu, HI

Japanese Americans Relocated During World War II — Yaeko C Tsutsui
1941 - California, United States
RESIDENCE San Francisco, California

U.S. City Directories, 1822-1995 — May T Territorial C Tsutsui
RESIDENCE 1969 - Honolulu, Hawaii

U.S. City Directories, 1822-1995 — Judith K Tsutsui

ancestry

Judy Mae Puahaunani Tsutsui
in the U.S., Social Security Death Index, 1935-2014

No Image
text only collection

Request copy of
original application

Add alternate
information

Report issue

Name	Judy Mae Puahaunani Tsutsui
Last Residence	96744 Kaneohe, Honolulu, Hawaii
Born	15 Mar 1943
Died	2 Dec 2009
State (Year) SSN issued	Hawaii (1959)

SAVE Cancel

Write a comment

Make a Connection

Find others who are researching
Judy Mae Puahaunani Tsutsui in
Public Member Trees

Source Citation
Issue State: *Hawaii*; Issue Date: *1959*

Source Information
Ancestry.com. U.S., *Social Security Death Index, 1935-2014* [database on-line]. Provo, UT,
USA: Ancestry.com Operations Inc, 2011.

Original data: Social Security Administration. *Social Security Death Index, Master File.*
Social Security Administration.

Description
The Social Security Administration Death Master File contains information on millions
of deceased individuals with United States social security numbers whose deaths were
reported to the Social Security Administration. Birth years for the individuals listed
range from 1875 to last year. Information in these records includes name, birth date,
death date, and last known residence. Learn more...

ancestry

Wanda Lene Cooper

in the U.S., Social Security Applications and Claims Index, 1936-2007

No Image
Text-only collection

✎ Add alternate Information

⚠ Report issue

Name	Wanda Lene Cooper
	[Wanda Len Carroll]
	[Wanda Carroll]
SSN	576568064
Gender	Female
Race	White
Birth Date	30 Jun 1948
Birth Place	Honolulu, Hawaii
Death Date	2 May 2000
Type of Claim	Original SSN.
Notes	Jul 1966: Name listed as WANDA LENE COOPER; Sep 1968: Name listed as WANDA LEN CARROLL; 08 Jun 2000: Name listed as WANDA CARROLL

SAVE ∨   Cancel

Suggested Records   ❓

☐ U.S., Social Security Death Index, 1935-2014
Wanda Carroll

☐ Tennessee, State Marriages, 1780-2002
Wanda Olene Cooper

☐ U.S. Public Records Index, 1950-1993, Volume 1
Wanda Cooper

☐ California, Passenger and Crew Lists, 1882-1959
Chaplene Cooper

☐ Web: Obituary Daily Times Index, 1995-Current
Wanda Lee (brooks) Carroll

☐ Honolulu, Hawaii, Passenger and Crew Lists, 1900-1959
Charlene Cooper

Source Information

Ancestry.com. U.S., Social Security Applications and Claims Index, 1936-2007 [database on-line]. Provo, UT, USA: Ancestry.com Operations, Inc., 2015.

Original data: Social Security Applications and Claims, 1936-2007.

Description

This database picks up where the SSDI leaves off, with details such as birth date and parents' names extracted from information filed with the Social Security Administration through the application or claims process. Learn more...

Write a comment.

Make a Connection

Find others who are researching Wanda Lene Cooper in Public Member Trees

ancestry

All Birth, Marriage & Death results for
Wanda Lene Cooper Carroll

Wanda Lene
Cooper Carroll
BORN 1947
LIVED Waikane, Ho...

COLLECTION   All Collections

Edit Search   New Search

All Categories

Birth, Marriage & Death

Birth, Baptism &
Christening

Marriage & Divorce

Death, Burial, Cemetery
& Obituaries

Shortcut Keys ►

Results 1–20 of 70,539

U.S., Social Security Applications
and Claims Index, 1936-2007
DEATH, BURIAL, CEMETERY & OBITUARIES

U.S., Social Security Death Index,
1935-2014
DEATH, BURIAL, CEMETERY & OBITUARIES

Texas Birth Index, 1903-1997
BIRTH, BAPTISM & CHRISTENING

View Image

U.S., Social Security Death Index,
1935-2014
DEATH, BURIAL, CEMETERY & OBITUARIES

California, Marriage Index, 1960-
1985
MARRIAGE & DIVORCE

View Image

Texas, Marriage Index, 1814-1909
and 1966-2011
MARRIAGE & DIVORCE

Texas, Divorce Index, 1968-2011
MARRIAGE & DIVORCE

RECORDS   CATEGORIES

NAME **Wanda Lene Cooper**
BIRTH 30 Jun 1948 - Honolulu,
Hawaii
DEATH 2 May 2000

NAME **Wanda Carroll**
BIRTH 30 Jun 1948
DEATH 2 May 2000
CIVIL Hawaii

NAME **Wanda Lynn Carroll**
BIRTH 28 Jul 1947 - Angelina

NAME **Wanda L. Carroll**
BIRTH 22 Nov 1946
DEATH 15 May 2007
CIVIL Oklahoma

NAME **Wanda L Cooper**
SPOUSE Lorenzo Leggett
BIRTH abt 1947
MARRIAGE 12 Mar 1971 - Los Angeles
City

NAME **Wanda L Cooper**
SPOUSE Billy E Etheridge
BIRTH abt 1947
MARRIAGE 22 May 1970 - Dallas

NAME **Wanda L Carroll**
SPOUSE Rodger D Carroll
BIRTH abt 1948
MARRIAGE 11 Aug 1966
DIVORCE 1 Jun 1981 - Lamar

NAME **Wanda L Carroll**

Marines' Plan for Jungle Training In Waikane Valley Reopens Old Wounds

posted in: May 2003 | 0

Waging pretend war is becoming popular on O`ahu's lush northeastern landscape. In the last couple of years, war movies starring Nicholas Cage and Bruce Willis, filmed at Kualoa and Waikane, made rubber-neckers out of anyone driving the winding two-lane road up Ko`olauloa. Pyrotechnics blew by day and bright camera lights glowed at night.

Now the U.S. Marines want in – or, rather, back in, to be precise.

While some believe the proposed explosive-free jungle warfare training will be far less disruptive than the movies, many in the rural community around Waikane have some unfinished business with the military. Decades of artillery training on land leased to the Marines by the Kamaka family left the land contaminated with ordnance. When the family tried to force the military to clean it up, as lease terms required, the Department of Defense instead condemned the land. The cost of cleaning up the land for unrestricted use was, the DOD said, many times higher than purchasing it outright. Now, more than a decade after the condemnation, the Marines want to resume training at Waikane.

The proposal has struck a raw nerve among the Kamaka family, area residents and the wider community of activists who are pressing for the restoration not only of Waikane, but of Makua Valley in West O`ahu, the island of Kaho`olawe, and other areas in the islands where the military's scars on the land run deep.

The Marines are in the process of conducting an environmental assessment for the jungle training plan, first disclosed last July. While the EA is not the full-blown environmental impact statement that the community has asked for, the Marines are seeking out public comment in a way that is unusual for a standard EA.

"There was a consensus [among community representatives] that you need to have a public meeting where people can come to hear each other," says June Cleghorn, a cultural resource specialist at the Marine Corps Base Hawai`i.

How that concession to the community will influence the outcome remains to be seen. A draft EA is expected in June or July, according a Marine Corps spokesperson.

What's on the Table

Preparing the EA is Honolulu firm Wil Chee – Planning Inc., with help from a handful of other local contractors studying the proposed action's effects on terrestrial and aquatic biology, water and air quality, archaeology, traffic, socio-economics, environmental justice, and noise.

What exactly do the Marines have in mind?

For a few days two to three times a month, 100 to 150 Marines will board as many as four buses at Kane`ohe Marine Base, zip across H-3, and then follow the winding route up the two-lane Kamehameha Highway to Waikane. On "rare" occasions, they'll make the 25-minute trip in Humvees or seven-ton trucks. Once parked, they'll walk up the gravel and dirt road to the training area, where they'll split into platoons and squads, according to informational materials on the proposed action.

While sporadic use will be the norm, military documents state that the Marines may occasionally use the area for two months straight, "to meet mission requirements." Sometimes, the place will be left alone for up to two months. At the training area, troops will learn how to navigate streams, ridges, and dense foliage, while avoiding fake mines and booby traps, according to a summary of actions. They'll also practice hostage rescue and attacking each other with blanks, chalk bullets, paintball, or laser guns. Reconnaissance through tree-climbing and rappelling down the valley ridges is also part of the plan.

The MCBH emphasizes that no aviation or mechanized support will be involved and that no live fire will be used. Prohibiting live fire weapons and ammunition "was an important concession to make to the surrounding communities," said Major Chris Hughes, public affairs director for the Marine Corps Base Hawaiʻi, in a press release last year. The training, he concluded, was "exceedingly important now, post 9/11."

Two years ago, the Islamic militant group Abu Sayyaf took two American missionaries and a Filipino nurse hostage in the jungles of Basilan Island, in the Philippines. American troops from Hawaiʻi flew in to help hunt the guerrillas, but returned saying that they were inadequately prepared for operating in thick jungle. Since Waikane has a "triple-canopy" jungle, similar to that in the Philippines, the Marines decided to revive the old training ground. That, at least, is the account offered by the Marines.

However, the idea that Marines need to train for operations in the Philippines is disputed by the Demilitarize Hawaiʻi — Aloha ʻAina Campaign (associated with American Friends Service Committee, or AFSC, a Quaker organization). A flier it distributed notes that Filipinos erupted in "massive protests" against the intervention of U.S. troops in the Philippines, making their further use there unlikely. In addition, the flier says, "the Philippines' constitution prohibits foreign military operations in the Philippines."

Once a Farm

Ten years have passed since District Court Judge Samuel King approved the government's condemnation of the Kamaka family land. Raymond Kamaka, who was the last Kamaka to farm the land, can now only watch as the jungle overtakes places he once cared for. He sometimes makes the trip up Waikane Valley Road to gather and visit the sacred heiau named after his great-great grandfather, Kahukukala, which sits on a ridge overlooking the Waikane Taro Flats, a site Raymond's father, Ronald, had registered as one of the nation's historic sites to protect it.

A flimsy wire fence that runs along the proposed training area, posted with danger and keep-out signs, is supposed to deter people from coming in, but on the weekends, Raymond says, "It's nothing but dirtbikers and pig hunters."

But what really bothers Raymond is that his neighbors, who are "ten steps from our property line," are still able to farm. "They found bombs on their land. But [the government] didn't stop them from farming," he says.

Although many people trespass within the off-limits area, the jungle-training proposal flies in the face of everything the public and the Kamakas had been led to believe about the hazards buried within the 187-acre parcel, part of a larger Waiahole-Waikane training area.

Through World War II up until the 1960s, the military shot up and bombed land it leased from the McCandless and Kamaka families, which had controlled the area since at least the early 1900s. Under the lease terms, the military was supposed to have restored the land to its original condition and remove all ammunition, shells and explosives when the lease ended. The lease also required that the military replant the impact area.

In June 1976, Colonel Robert E. Switzer of the U.S. Marine Corps informed the Kamakas that the U.S. government had fulfilled its lease terms, and that the property was "free of ordnance hazards, well covered with vegetation and in good state of police." The Kamakas, however, found the area was littered with shell casings and explosion craters. So from August to September 1976, the Marines cleared the land of 24,400 pounds of ordnance and scrap. A report of the cleanup concluded that the area's heavy vegetation, rough terrain, steep slope, and embedded shells made it impossible to certify the land as ordnance-free.

Ignorant of the USMC's conclusion, the Kamakas lived and farmed on 30 acres of their property for several years without incident, digging with plows and tractors to depths of more than five feet at times. But in December 1983, heavy rains exposed thousands of unexploded rounds on the property. A military sweep that month yielded 480 3.5-inch rockets.

On January 18, 1984, the U.S. Marines prepared a preliminary environmental assessment for ordnance removal. To clear the Waikane parcel, a series of up to 2,000 rounds would have to be detonated, one at a time over 90 days, to set off the potentially explosive ordnance buried within the parcel. The environmental impacts, the preliminary EA states, would be noise and vibrations during explosions, minor vegetation damage and one-and-a-half to two-foot wide craters, six to eight inches deep. The EA noted that there would be some damage to the Kamaka family shrine, as well. To do the cleanup, a state Conservation District Use Permit would have been needed, since part of the land is within the state Conservation District.

In February 1984, the Army, Marine Corps, Navy and Air Force began a three-month cleanup of the area over 85 percent of the property's surface. The effort yielded 16,000 pounds of ordnance. The rest of the land, which was covered with vegetation, and all underground ordnance remained untouched.

After the cleanup, Raymond says, he threw a thank-you party at the Kane`ohe Marine Base, killing one of his pigs for the event. To his surprise, however, finding that it would be too costly to continue, the Marines gave up on the clean-up effort and began condemnation proceedings – a move that the Kamakas would fight in court.

Condemnation

Congress authorized the property's purchase in November 1986, and in January 1989, the military filed its for condemnation and deposited a check for $735,000, the estimated amount of compensation, in an account. The Kamaka family filed its opposition that June.

U.S. District Court Judge David Ezra found that the military had not proved that it couldn't clear the land practically and at reasonable cost, and allowed the military time to determine whether that was possible. The case was later given to Judge King, who, on June 16, 1993, after reviewing the results of the government's surveys and studies, ruled that the U.S. government had proved that Kamakas' land was so contaminated with unexploded ordnance that it had no choice but to condemn it.

Judge King's Findings of Fact (FOF) states that for about two-and-a-half weeks in June 1990, the Naval Explosive Ordnance Disposal Technology Center had tested its ability to clear the land using available technology. The FOF states that 75MM shells could have penetrated as deep as 100 inches into the soil – too deep for the military's best metal detectors, which can only detect shells embedded in the soil as far as 40 inches deep.

Clearing ordnance that lay deeper "could only be achieved by clearing the property of all vegetation and then either removing enough earth to get the ordnance items within the range of he locators or by mass soil processing," the FOF states. "Either method would cause destruction to the environment."

If the Kamakas wanted to farm, recreate and construct sheds, pipelines, and the like, the land would have to be cleaned to a depth of at least 10 feet. And even then, there would still be the risk of future exposure by erosion or disturbance, the FOF states.

Cleanup would not only be impractical, King wrote, it would also cost too much. The property's estimated market value, $735,000, was a pittance compared to the $5.8 million it would cost to do a shallow clearing, one to two feet deep, or the $7.3 million it would take to do a slightly deeper one, one to four feet deep.

A Settlement

All of the 30-plus Kamaka family heirs, except for Raymond and McRonald Kamaka, accepted the court's judgment (although McRonald did sign on years later). "We couldn't disprove that it wasn't that bad," says Judy Tsutsui, one of the Kamaka family heirs. After the initial ruling by King allowing condemnation, the next phase was to determine a fair market value that all parties could agree on. The Kamakas felt their property was worth much more than the initial $735,000 the government had proposed.

Tsutsui and Leroy Chung, both Kamaka family heirs, suggested that the land could be valued anywhere from $5 million to $14 million, considering the fact that the family could have built many homes on the property.

The Kamaka family brought in Davianna McGregor of the University of Hawai`i to relay to the government the importance of ancestral lands to native Hawaiians. The government dismissed her testimony, saying it had nothing to do with appraisal. In the end, the family agreed to a sum of $2,099,922 for their property, except for the lo`i and the heiau, which they felt were too sacred ever to be sold.

According to the May 1994 agreement that laid out the final settlement terms, the family could regain title to the property if the Secretary of the Navy decided it was able to clear the property of all explosive hazards, and if Congress appropriated the money to do so. Title to the property, or a portion of it, would be returned to family members who provided written consent to the reconveyance and agreed to pay the fair market value of the land at the time of taking — $1.75 million plus interest — or fair market value at the time of resale, whichever amount was lower.

The agreement also states that every 10 years, the Kane`ohe Marine Corps Air Station's Explosive Ordnance Disposal personnel must assess whether it's feasible to clean the area.

"The United States and the Defendants recognize that the probable presence of unexploded ordnance on the subject property presents a danger to those who enter the property," the agreement stated. But acknowledging the Kamaka family's ties to the land, the agreement allows the Kamakas three visits a year for as long as three hours each to the ahu (shrine) and the lo`i, solely for cultural or religious purposes. Visitors, as many as ten at a time, must be escorted by Kane`ohe Marine base Explosive Ordnance Division personnel, and must all be named defendants in the case or their lineal descendants, and be 15 years old or older. Visitors must provide written notice of their intent to visit 10 days ahead of time.

Throughout the trial, Raymond Kamaka never wavered in his opposition, stating that the Kingdom of Hawai`i still exists, making the condemnation process illegal. He also refused to pay his federal taxes, which landed in him in jail from 1993 to 1995.

"The news media made like it was tax evasion and postal fraud, but I was fighting to save my land," he told *Environment Hawai`i*. "The fine print was that I was harassing the governmentÉ.[But] after I got out, I got an apology from the government."

In August 1994, after the rest of his family had agreed to a settlement, Raymond wrote to King from federal prison in California that since he had not signed or agreed to the settlement, the court should not distribute the settlement money. Distribution can come about only after all parties named in the dispute over our family's ancestral land have signed, he wrote, adding that he would be lodging his case with the United Nations' Human Rights Committee.

Because of Raymond's resistance, the case remains open and status conferences with Judge King and attorneys from both sides continue. At a 1998 status conference, Judge King told the parties that "this case has Hawaiian problems and cannot be closed out at this time." In subsequent status conferences, Raymond expressed that he did not want his $60,000 portion of the settlement, but wanted his land back. The next status conference is scheduled for October 17, 2003.

Reaching Out

"I still have my property as far as I'm concerned," Raymond says. But when he found out about the Marine Corps' plan to resume training, he was stunned.

"Somehow the land cleaned itself up and they can come back in. We never had too much people up there, mostly farmers. Now there are bike riders, pakalolo growers, DOFAW [state Division of Forestry and Wildlife] and hunters. There was supposed to have been an eight-foot fence with barbed wire to keep people out" — a shibai, he says. Now with the jungle training proposal, he says, "Some of the family felt, 'What is going on?'"

Tsutsui says when she found out, "It didn't surprise me that they would pull that. There they go again."

Against this history, the Marine Corps knew its proposal to begin sending hundreds of troops to tromp around Waikane every month would be met with outrage.

Last August, shortly after news of the jungle training broke, Hughes, the public affairs director for the Marines in Hawai`i, briefed the Kahalu`u Neighborhood Board.

Immediately, he was asked the obvious question: if the land is not safe for the Kamakas to use, how can it be safe for Marines? To this, Hughes replied that an environmental assessment would help discover what hazards are still there and if it's found to be too dangerous, "the game is over."

One resident at the Neighborhood Board meeting said that condemning land that the Marines had promised – but failed – to care for was the same as stealing it. If the land was safe enough to conduct training, he said, it could be safe enough to return.

Some board members believed that an EA was a waste of time and that the Marines should immediately begin preparing an environmental impact statement, including a cultural impact statement. In addition, the board discussed the idea that among the alternatives considered in the environmental assessment, the Marines should give as much weight to clean-up and return of the land to farming as it did to use of the land as a training area.

In the end, the board voted to ask the Marines for an EIS that would include "an assessment of restoration opportunities for environmental, cultural, and social values associated with the whole ahupua`a." It also asked for funds that would allow the community to hire its own consultants for an independent evaluation of the planning documents.

Despite this vote, the Marines have kept with their plan to produce a less comprehensive environmental assessment. No decision had been made by mid-April as to what alternative actions to lay out in the document (other than the no-action alternative), but cleaning the unexploded ordinance from the land was not among options being considered, sources told *Environment Hawai'i*.

Around the time of the neighborhood board meeting, Major Robert Rouse, in charge of shepherding the jungle training plan through the National Environmental Policy Act (NEPA) process, was quietly gathering input from individuals in the Waikane community — a tactic that, according to Kahalu'u Neighborhood Board president Amy Luersen, only served to deepen suspicion.

Raymond Kamaka says he didn't find out about the proposal until someone called him saying, "Did you know the military is having meetings with WWCA [the Waiahole-Waikane Community Association], trying to get on people's good side in the community?" The meetings, which were indeed held, were "with the wrong people," he adds, "mostly lessees, not landowners…none of them know the real story of Waikane mountain."

Taking advice from Luersen and others, the Marines agreed to create a Community Advisory Group with members of the Kahalu'u Neighborhood Board, area legislators and others. The group would advise the Marines on how to address the broader community.

The first product of that group was a community meeting held at Windward Community College March 5. Comments made during that meeting, the Marines promised, would be addressed in the environmental assessment and posted on the EA website. Such extensive public participation, they stressed, goes beyond what is required for an EA.

That evening, Major Rouse received a non-stop verbal blasting from some of East O'ahu's preeminent environmental and cultural watchdogs. Most of the attendees were adamant that the military needed to clean the lands it contaminates.

A Filipino graduate student at the University of Hawai'i protested the justification the Marines were offering to reopen Waikane. U.S. military involvement the Philippines violated the country's sovereignty and destabilized the peace process there, she said, adding that the expense of reopening Waikane simply to train soldiers so they can eradicate a few hundred guerrillas was outrageous.

Because he dealt only with fulfilling the requirements of the National Environmental Policy Act, Rouse said, he couldn't speak to the foreign policy of the United States. But under NEPA, he said, a need only has to be stated, not justified, adding, "There is a continuing requirement to have jungle training. The Philippines is just an example."

Others, like Cathy Mattoon of the Punalu'u Community Association, didn't believe the Marines needed "one more square foot!" According to the Demilitarize Hawaii – Aloha 'Aina Campaign, nearly a quarter of the island of O'ahu is controlled by the military. Kyle Kajihiro, who spoke at the meeting and works with the AFSC's Honolulu office, told *Environment Hawai'i*, "The pattern has been whenever the U.S. is at war, it uses the occasion to acquire more land in Hawai'i."

Paul Reppun, a taro farmer from Waiahole, said at the March meeting, "I don't care if you go in there with bedroom slippers," if the land can be farmed, it should be put to that use immediately.

Yet another testifier told the Marines to, "grow your own jungle."

The testimony was music to Raymond's ears. Not one to make a loud fuss out of respect for his family, Raymond says he had long felt like he was alone in his fight and was "so happy" to hear his position acknowledged by others in his community.

The strong community opposition was enough for John Morgan of nearby Kualoa Ranch to withdraw an offer he made last year to the Marines to look at the ranch as an alternative in case Waikane could not be used.

Cleanup

At the March meeting, some people felt the land could be opened up to the public if it was safe enough for Marines to stomp around. Rouse, however, responded that the land was still unsafe for unrestricted public use, which might include farming and digging.

"Marines have a different standard of safety," he said.

Tsutsui says, "At that meeting, what I didn't have a chance to say was they kept telling us-and this is not in the records, it was pre-court time when they were trying to get us to accept the $735000-they kept telling us they wouldn't put one of their soldiers back on there again," because it was so unsafe.

When someone asked Rouse if he thought the Kamakas had been wronged, Rouse was booed when he said no. He added afterwards that it is Congress' place, not his, to issue apologies. Rouse also rejected the idea of cleaning the area under the current NEPA process.

Despite the community's sentiments, Rouse's position is "going to hold," says Cleghorn, whose supervisor is Rouse. The current EA is only looking at the proposed action, not cleanup, "but that doesn't mean it's never going to happen," she says. "It's just not going to happen under MCBH process."

"If you look at the military's history in Hawai'i, it stinks," she continues, and the "legal technicalities" that led to the condemnation of the Kamaka land were "unfortunate."

Except for Rouse, she notes, all of those involved in preparing the EA live in Hawai'i. "We don't like the fact we can't clean it up, either," she says. "We knew that was going to be one of the first things that came up. One of the family members stood up [at the March meeting] saying, 'You want to dirty this valley, why don't you clean it?' People at the Marine base are very sympathetic to that. It's a no-win situation in terms of cleaning. We say, 'Go to your congressmen.' You hate to hear that," she says, but that's what will be required to get the valley cleaned.

On the other hand, suggestions the advisory group have made to require water quality testing, allow restoration of ancient sites and access to cultural sites by the public, Hawaiians, and school groups, are "definite possibilities," Cleghorn says.

Raymond Kamaka continues his resistance to the condemnation. "When you make a promise to the kupunas (elders), you don't go back on that," he says. As for the MCBH's plan to do jungle training, "I pray on it," he says, "and let the Lord take care of business."

To comment or to find out more on the EA, visit [url=http://www.mcbh.usmc.mil/EA/ea_home.htm]www.mcbh.usmc.mil/EA/ea_home.htm[/url] For background on the Kamaka condemnation, look up the August 1992 issue of Environment Hawai'i

— Teresa Dawson

Volume 13, Number 11 May 2003

About the author

David Earl Kaleoikaika Cooper and his beautiful wife, Katherine Sachie Arakaki Cooper, married for fifty-five years, live alternately in Honolulu, Hawaii and Old Town, Alexandria, Virginia; the proud parents of Troy, Brad and Ethan, and truly proud Grandparents of Ikaika, Kekoa, Kawehi and Kapono, they served our country for thirty years on active duty when the author retired as a Brigadier General, U.S. Army in November 1993.

In November 1993 the author founded and served as the President of the Pacific American Foundation, a national 501(c)(3) dedicated to improving the well-being of all Pacific Americans - American Samoans, Chamorros, Fijians, Maoris, Native Hawaiians, Tahitians and Tongans – who as American citizens share their proud cultures of the Pacific with other citizens of our country.

In November 2004 the author stepped down as President of The Pacific American Foundation in order to form and lead the Native Hawaiian Organization (NHO), Hui O Hana Pono, consisting today of eight companies whose capabilities range from missile engineering to S/TS armed and escort security to base facilities to landscaping to tree trimming to real estate and to wealth management with contracts and more than seven hundred employees in fifteen states.

The author remains involved with fund raising for the Roll Call of Honor, Children with Cancer, Buffalo Soldiers Memorial at the United States Military Academy, Hui Scholars Program, Royal Hawaiian Academy of Traditional Arts and with several other community organizations.

He and his wife remain involved with life through their children, grandchildren, fitness, work, travel and community participation.

www.ingramcontent.com/pod-product-compliance
Lightning Source LLC
Chambersburg PA
CBHW071348280526
45787CB00001B/250